How To Fly Like An Eagle With Wings Like A Wimp!

Since Greatness Is Possible Excellence Is Not Enough!

Go For Greatness!

Jonas Gadson, DTM

Known As "Mr. Enthusiastic"

Jonas Gadson 2011

Partners for Purposeful Living Publishing Company
Beaufort, South Carolina

First printing 2010
ISBN 978-0-9829379-3-8
LCCN 2010935038

ATTENTION CORPORATIONS, UNIVERSITIES, COL-LEGES, AND PROFESSIONAL ORGANIZATIONS: Quantity discounts are available on bulk purchases of this book for educational, gift purposes, or as premiums for increasing magazine subscriptions or renewals. Special books or book excerpts can also be created to fit specific needs. For information, please contact Partners for Purposeful Living Publishing Company, P.O. Box 629, Beaufort, SC 29901-0629; (843) 838-3853; jg@jonasbonus.com.

Table of Contents

"How To Fly Like An Eagle With Wings Like A Wimp!"

Jonas Gadson Unlimited
A Corporate Training Company
Specializing in
Speaking, Training and Developing Greatness!

Jonas Gadson, DTM

Jonas Gadson, DTM - known as "Mr. Enthusiastic!"
is a Nationally-Known Motivational Speaker, Certified Trainer,
Consultant, Radio Personality, Author and Ordained Minister!
He is President and CEO of
Jonas Gadson Unlimited – A Corporate Training Company.
He is committed to helping people develop
their personal and professional Greatness!

We understand that the economy is challenging and difficult right now
"But don't focus on what you have lost...Focus on what you have left...
Because what you have left is enough to get the job done!"
Get tried, tested techniques and proven skills that will help you
Achieve "Your Dreams, Your Goals, and Your Aspirations!"

If you are looking for a Speaker for your Next Event
Call "Mr. Enthusiastic!"
He will Electrify your Audience
He is a Trainer to Transform your Team
A Champion to Charge your Team to Victory
A Master in Communication to Motivate your Mentors, Management & Members
A Leader to Lift Up your Board of Directors, Corporate and Business leaders
A Partner with a Positive message to Prepare you for Success and Significance
A Coach to Create the Environment to "Educate, Inspire and Motivate" YOU
Call NOW And Get YOUR Bonus From Jonas!
His Motto Is: "Since Greatness Is Possible Excellence Is Not Enough!
Go For Greatness!"

He has "Educational, Inspirational and Motivational" messages for YOU!
Get his new book: "How To Fly Like An Eagle With Wings Like A Wimp!"
Get your CDs, DVDs, Videos and cassettes of his signature speech of the same title,
delivered to 500 people from around the world and other Motivational Material.
Call him NOW at (843) 838-3853 or (843) 379-8145
jg@jonasbonus.com • www.jonasbonus.com
Or write Jonas Gadson Unlimited • P.O. Box 629 Beaufort, South Carolina 29901- 0629

Here Is What People Are Saying About Jonas Gadson...

Mr. Gadson presented "How to Give A Powerful Presentation!" in Randolph, MA, designed for all who have a message to deliver. It was sensational! Dr. Dawna L. Jones, MD said, "I felt empowered...confident to give my upcoming lecture...I am excited about what I was able to learn and can incorporate right away."

"I have attended numerous conferences, workshops, seminars and training sessions conducted by Mr. Jonas Gadson. I see why he is known as 'Mr. Enthusiastic!' I am in awe at how he always exceeds at delivering 'powerful, positive and purposeful presentations' that are always resounding, relevant, and renewing! I can hardly wait for his new book, *How To Fly Like An Eagle With Wings Like A Wimp!* I highly recommend you to book him as your next Keynote Speaker, Leadership Trainer, or Motivational Speaker! I guarantee that you will never be the same!"—Dr. Dale Chanaiwa, Founder of Diamond Dale Discoveries, "Encouraging, Inspiring and Empowering" Women to Passionately Pursue Their greatness!

He addressed the membership of the New England Minority Supplier Development Council. Ms. Tina Andrews, past president said this: "Mr. Jonas Gadson was exceptional! The excitement and motivation created by his presentation has you feeling like you actually do have a pair of wings! It leaves you believing that you can do just about anything!"

One of the participants from his "How to Fly Like an Eagle..." Seminar in Boston, Ms. Tiffanie Williams, president of her own marketing and PR firm had this to say: "Mr. Jonas Gadson is a talented speaker who really knows how to ignite inspiration and the passion of possibilities that is within us all!"

Of his seminar on "Build High and Healthy Self-Esteem," educator and principal of Fletcher Academy, Ms. Robin Harris said, "Mr. Jonas Gadson is a fabulous speaker! I have even listened to my CD 'How to Fly Like an Eagle...' when I am (in my car) driving to work!"

Photographer Mrs. Gretje Ferguson said, "I just want to thank you for the enlightening seminar... I came away inspired and energized, with a new clarity about what I need to do... You two are a great team...I'm flying like an eagle!"

"It is a privilege to know that you continue to grow the business! ...I can't believe that a year has gone by. But I do remember at the beginning of the year attending your workshop, 'How to Fly Like an Eagle' and it was the perfect motivational springboard! In January, when I take the time to review my goals and successes I know that I flew high like an eagle at least most of the time (this year!)"—Mrs. Mary Fernandes, MBTA, Assistant General Manager. Silver Line

"How to Fly Like an Eagle!"...How to soar above the clouds! How to maintain a constant and safe altitude! Wow! What a fantastic seminar! Mr.Gadson stimulated the intimate gathering of professionals to a new state of consciousness. After this infusion of enthusiasm, I can identify areas within that need to be addressed and toxic immaturity jettison. This cleansing has enabled me to safely achieve the desired altitude without substantial drag from internal unrest. Mr. Gadson showed me 'How to Fly Like An Eagle' by clearing the flight deck of internal clutter; thus making the flight instruments for obtaining and maintaining a smooth flight, clearly visible."—Mr. Javier Jackson, Boston Public Schools

Mrs. Paige Stover-Hague, host of her own radio program, Financially Speaking Radio, indicated that she loves "the Bonus From Jonas!" This is a short, descriptive phrase designed to get you to "get up and go!"

"Once in awhile someone comes along in life that you recognize right away as a person who is capable of having a tremendous impact on your life and that of others. Jonas Gadson is one such individual. After hearing Jonas speak I recommended him as a speaker for the South Carolina National Eligibility Workers Association's (SCNEW) Fall Workshop. The SCNEW Board selected Jonas, and he presented at our workshop! The topic was, 'A New Way to Say Yes to Your Success!' It was the first time that a speaker came to our organization and received a standing ovation! Jonas' witty and colorful presentation gave SCNEW organization members and guests a plethora of ideas to enhance our professional and personal success! Thanks Jonas...You Are a REAL Bonus!"—Ms. Shearl Jones, former president of the board, South Carolina National Eligibility Workers Association (SCNEW)

Mrs. Dora Burton, partner and director of business development with Burton RE Associates, said, "I love the Bonus From Jonas! This is not my first time and I would do it again! The information is helpful and very motivating..."

Ms. Glenda Williams, program coordinator with the American Red Cross of Rochester, said, "As the program coordinator of the American Red Cross, it is my privilege to spread the word of our Nation's best kept secret! I highly recommend you, Jonas Gadson, to perform motivational speaking, educational and leadership training to youth and adult groups in non-profit, private and corporate settings. I make this recommendation because I have seen your work outside of the Red Cross, in other settings, working with different levels of the community!"

Mrs. Wilnetta Grant, retail sales manager with Sprint PCS, North Charleston, said, "I recently spoke to Mike Mullis about having this dynamic speaker to deliver for our proposed Managers' Rally/Summit in the near future. I normally do not send any emails to the executive levels but I feel this email is worth your consideration and investigation. I've had the privilege of hearing Mr. Jonas Gadson two weekends ago and he has motivated me to a higher level! His level of excitement and enthusiasm is something that the entire Alamosa company could benefit from; from our executive level to our front-line employees. I know we are moving toward the last quarter of the year... If in the near future Alamosa is in need of a corporate level trainer of greatness who would help move us closer to our goal of being the Employer of Choice, I strongly and highly recommend Mr. Jonas 'Enthusiastic!' Gadson."

"I believed that I had reached the pinnacle of success when I was at the bank in corporate America. Working with Mr. Jonas Gadson has shown me that I had only scratched the surface. The personal and professional transformation that I have experienced and witnessed in our seminar attendees says it all! Mr. Gadson has the skill, knowledge, and commitment to serve as a powerful transformational agent for those who dare take the journey to personal and professional greatness!"—Sidrah R. Jackson, Gadson-Jackson Productions

Mr.Gadson presented a three-hour professional development workshop to 75 professional health care counselors with the Orangeburg, South Carolina, Department of Mental Health. All had a minimum of a Masters Degree in order to counsel at that level. He spoke to a diverse audience who now wants to buy his new book *How To Fly Like An Eagle With Wings Like A Wimp!* And he received a standing ovation! Mrs. Bessie Abraham, the executive director who hired him said, "You superseded all of our expectations!" The organization is highlighting his training in their internal newsletter.

"Just wanted you to know how much I enjoyed your 'life lessons.' You have a gift of capturing the audience and holding them in the palm of your hands..."—Yvonne Smith Reeder, DTM

Business owner and architect Ms. Anaezi Modu said: "Powerful points! Acknowledges where you are! Provides Hope! Helps in your personal relationships as well!"

Motivational speaker and business owner of two beauty

salons in the beauty and retail industry, Mrs. Patricia Mavrides had this to say: "I love to see another person speaking from the heart!...My style!"

Mr. Gadson delivered a mini-seminar on Communication to the Beaufort/Jasper County Chapter of the South Carolina Healthcare Managers Association. (SCHMA) Organization president Ms. Stacey Bartlow wrote, "Thank you for your time and talent... You were fantastic!"

Ms. Cindy Ott, executive director of SCHMA in Columbia, SC, said, "Mr. Gadson is an Excellent Speaker!" Ms. Sharon Poston said, "I loved it! It was very motivational and inspirational! I wish I had a tape of it. I would listen to it all the time!"

Ms. Lucy Perez, former administrator for Global Family Medicine and whose son is a doctor, said, "What I liked the best was the story about the old man and the boy!"

Ms. Jane McKee, Hilton Head Hospital, said, "This was a positive presentation. Everyone can learn something!"

"It is with pleasure... Just to let you know that I recorded that Sunday morning service and I listen to it often because when I hear your voice and your word it just lifts my spirit. God has given you a gift which is only afforded to a chosen few so I am honoured that I've had the privilege of experiencing the Bonus in Jonas the gift God bestowed on you. Let me know when you finish your book I would like to purchase a copy. Blessing and favour from the United Kingdom."—Ms. Shirley Husbands, teacher, London, England

"Jonas Gadson, our minister, a man full of faith, vision, grace, and integrity! We are certainly proud of your accomplishments and your perseverance in getting the job done! We love You!"—Carla and John Boone, business owners and regional vice presidents with Primerica

Praise for Jonas Gadson
From Dottie Walters

Here is what Mrs. Dottie Walters, renowned speaker and former owner of *Sharing Ideas* magazine, founder of one of the largest professional speaker's bureaus in the world, and author of Speak and Grow Rich said about Jonas Gadson in "Speaker's Spotlight":

"Jonas Gadson: Entertaining! Fun! And Totally Unique! His new book is now completed. Wow! It is entitled, *How To Fly Like An Eagle With Wings Like A Wimp!* (How to climb the self-esteem mountain and stay at the summit.)

"Jonas has spoken for many top US companies such as Avon, Adelphi Automotive and many others. Eastman Kodak Company honored him with their 'Trainer of the Year' award for instructing over 8,000 employees representing over 69 countries (as part of a Three-Year Diversity Initiative).

"Keep your eyes on this man; he is flying with the eagles! Jonas often creates new words: For example, when he admires the accomplishments of women, he calls them 'Sheroes!' Sounds great. No wonder his clients call him 'Mr. Enthusiastic!'"

You Must Read This Book

How To Fly Like An Eagle With Wings Like A Wimp! is one book that you MUST read this year!

It is not for everybody but it is for anybody who is committed to personal and professional greatness! "You are next in line for a blessing! Don't get out of line, don't detour, and don't let anyone cut in front of you! It is full steam ahead!"

The eagle is the king of the air! It is a majestic bird. It is a symbol of courage, strength, and power. There is a direct correlation between the eagle and the human being. It has been said that the eagle is the only bird that doesn't head south during the winter. And when storms approach, the eagle refuses to run away from its storms. It prepares for them. It uses its skills to fly above the storm; instead of becoming a victim, it becomes a victor! Like the eagle, you too have the courage, strength and skills to live the life that you desire and you deserve!

I have written this book especially for you: To educate, to inspire, and to motivate you to live your dreams, your goals, and your aspirations! Maybe you are feeling a little down. Now is your time to mount up with wings like an Eagle (Isaiah 40:31) to "take a chance, take charge and take control of your life!" I will show you "how to turn your obstacles into opportunities; your stumbling blocks into stepping stones; your scars into stars!" And you will learn how to fly again. Not to focus on what you have lost, but to focus on what you have left! Because what you have left is enough to get the job done!

BONUS FROM JONAS
**"You have been divinely designed
and destined for greatness!"**

You are fearfully and wonderfully made! You will...learn how to fly, not to fall! How to climb, not to crawl! How to soar, not to sink! Prepare for the storms of life! Maybe it is the economy. Maybe you are unemployed; you are having health challenges, or relationship difficulties. Or maybe you are ready to move up to bigger and better things! "You can always Better Your Best!" This book is the answer for You!

How To Fly Like An Eagle With Wings Like A Wimp! will inspire you to "never give up, never give in, and to never give out! It is always too early to quit! Because a quitter never wins and a winner never quits!" Calling all eagles.

It's your time to mount up!

A Special Note From the Author to You

The title of this book is *How To Fly Like An Eagle With Wings Like A Wimp!*

I am aware that you are not an eagle, nor do you have wings! This terminology is used to create a metaphor to show you some of the similarities between eagles and human beings. In this book, I am clearly going to show you and explain to you through stories, illustrations, facts and strategies of overcoming trials the meaning of the first part of the book title, "How to Fly Like an Eagle..." and much more!

I am not speaking as an authority on eagles, but I am speaking as a person who has studied eagles through my personal, professional, historical, and spiritual interests and research.

Now I would like to explain what I mean when I refer to the second part of the book title, "With Wings Like a Wimp!"

I am not insinuating that you are a wimp. I wouldn't dare. Because I know you are an eagle! However, I am demonstrating that you were given capabilities, gifts, talents, and abilities just as the eagles were. When the eaglets are born, they don't know how to utilize their wings automatically. Neither do they know the purpose of their wings, which are undeveloped, small, and weak. In other words, the wings are in a wimpy condition. They aren't ready to be used yet. The eaglets have the potential to fly when they are born but their wings are weak, unused, and unproductive! The eaglets must be taught how to fly and to use their wings properly! It takes 10 to 12 weeks for the eaglets to become fully developed and reach their full wingspan of more than 16 inches.

Let me tell you a story: When I bought my first cellular telephone, I didn't know its full capabilities. I knew how to turn it on and I knew how to turn it off—and that's about it!

But my daughter showed me the variety of choices I had for the ring tone. She showed me how I could send and receive text messages. She demonstrated how I could use it as a camera and take a picture.

I had the telephone for a year before I knew all of its potential. Until then, I didn't know how to access its power and additional features. I was like the eaglet with all of its potential with wings. But I hadn't reached my full wingspan yet.

How many of you are like the eaglet and still don't understand how to use your abilities and skills?

How many of you are just like me with my new cellular telephone? You have the abilities, the education—the degrees! However, you still haven't achieved your purpose in life! I had already been carrying my telephone around for over a year without accessing its full capabilities. What is it positive that is in you that you have been carrying around inside of you and have not utilized it? When are you planning on maximizing your full potential? "We weren't designed to be carriers; we were designed to be producers!"

Sometimes, if we are not careful, we get caught up with status. All of these features on our telephones, in our homes, in our vehicles, in our lives, but we haven't fully utilized any of them! This is your time. It's not the time for "wimping." It is not the time for weeping. It's time for Winning! Just as my daughter came and showed me how to access the capabilities on my telephone which I had purchased but didn't know how to use—I didn't realize what I had in my hand nor did I know how to access its features! Just like me, this book will give you access to how you can reach your full potential and achieve your purpose. If you positively and wisely use what you have in your hand, you will *win!* You will be fully utilizing your potential. Living your purpose and Living it with a Passion! And you can start Right Now!

Bonus From Jonas
on Greatness

"Since Greatness Is Possible Excellence Is Not Enough! Go For Greatness!"

This is your time to stop surviving and start striving!

In this book I am going to set you up for success by showing you how to access your full potential that will help you to live your purpose with a passion! This book will help you to access your full potential.

You have heard it said, "Knowledge is power!" Knowledge is not power. Knowledge is potential power! It is there but being underutilized. It becomes power when it is put into practice.

BONUS FROM JONAS
"You have heard it said that practice brings about perfection. Practice doesn't bring about perfection; practice brings about improvement! You can always better your *best!*"

As a human being, you have many gifts. We understand that you are not literally an eagle. And that literally, you do not have wings. You have the potential to fly to heights you have never imagined when you implement your gifts and talents. This is a metaphor. In my book, I emphasize some positive qualities that both human beings and eagles possess as a way to "educate, inspire, and motivate."

Don't let your "wings" atrophy. (If you don't use it, you'll lose it!) This may sound like an oxymoron. If the wings are not fully developed, aren't being used to the optimum, you can have a lot of power without understanding how to use it.

Even when the eagles' wings are fully developed, if they don't know how to use them they cannot operate at their optimal power. If we don't use our knowledge, skills, and talents then we will lose them.

Because we haven't learned how to access our full potential and how to live our purpose with a passion, we are POOR. An acrostic that means:

Passing
Over
Opportunities
Repeatedly

Sometimes the reason we miss out on opportunities is because they come dressed in overalls and look too much like work. This is a state of mind.

BONUS FROM JONAS
"Don't focus on what you are going through; focus on what you are going to! If you know what you are going to it doesn't matter what you are going through!"

Congratulations on your wise decision to invest in the greatest person on the planet. You!
Welcome to
How To Fly Like An Eagle With Wings Like A Wimp!

BONUS FROM JONAS
**"There is no defense against greatness...
if there is a crack, then greatness will seep through...
if there is no crack, then greatness will
break through!"**

Introduction

**Traumatic Struggles, Tremendous Triumphs,
Transformed Future, and True Treasures!
Learning How to Fly and Finding My Wings!**

My name is Jonas Willie Gadson, and I am one of 11 children born to Joseph Christopher Gadson and Eliza Mary Gadson. I was born on September 13, 1953, on Tom Fripp plantation on St. Helena Island, South Carolina. Slavery had been abolished, but segregation was in full force. Despite the condition of segregation and discrimination, my mother worked very hard for her children to ensure that we would have a better life. She had the mindset that we would go to higher heights. And my mother believed that I was destined to be Great.

When I was a little boy, I was very sickly and my stomach was protruding out as if I was pregnant. If you have seen the commercials on television with the starving Ethiopian children, you observed how their bodies were skinny but their stomachs were big. This was how I was. My mother didn't know what was wrong. I was the sickest child out of all of my mother's children. But my mother was determined to find a cure for my health condition.

On St. Helena Island, often the midwives who delivered you provided care when you got sick. My Auntie Gal (Mary Owens) was a midwife who is now 104 years old, and she delivered hundreds of babies on the island. She had delivered me but my illness was way beyond her area of expertise and understanding. The midwives had exhausted all of their knowledge, skill, and remedies, and nothing worked. I didn't get better, I got worse. Then I was taken to Beaufort Hospital. I was taken to Beaufort Hospital during the time that the Jim Crow laws were still in effect in the South. Therefore, I didn't get the care I needed and they said that there was nothing that they could do for me.

Then I was rushed to Charleston, South Carolina, to Roper Hospital. Roper Hospital was the first community hospital in the Carolinas whose mission became to "treat the sick without regard to complexion, religion or nation." At the tender age of four, I had to undergo major surgery; my life was at stake. I had a tumor in my stomach that made it protrude out as if I were pregnant. The doctors at Roper Hospital told my mother they had operated on eight other babies who had the same condition I had, and all eight died. The doctors told my mother that I was going to die too. They operated on me as if I was not human. My mother, though, did not let me know the bleakness of the situation. Her iron will and strong faith sent me the message that "I would live." The doctors gave my mother a diagnosis that I was going to die, but God had the final prognosis, and His prognosis was that "Jonas is going to live." And here's your Bonus and you can only get this...

BONUS FROM JONAS
"Don't let anyone bury you until after you are dead. You are bigger than that. You are better than that and the *best* is still in you!"

I remember coming out of surgery, heavily sedated and in pain, stitches all in my stomach. When I lifted up my body with the little strength that I had, and looked over and down, I saw my mother sitting on a chair right by my side and she was so tired that she was sleeping. But she was right there by my side. Oh, what a powerful message of love and confidence this picture gave me. That picture is etched in my heart and in my mind forever. This was the commitment, love, and closeness I had with my mother. A good mother believes in you even during your toughest times.

However, I got an infection. I believe that my surgery was performed with the mindset of the doctors that I was going to die anyway. Perhaps they had hoped it would be a learning experience or they could donate my organs to save others. Perhaps the instruments they used were not sterile as a result. Regardless of the reason, the surgery created an even more life-threatening condition. And they had to operate again.

It was another surgery on my right side near my back. They made a deep incision to drain out the toxins that had developed from the infection from the first surgery. I had now been wounded in two different places on my body—my stomach and on my right side near my ribs and my back. That resulted in a very long journey on the road of recovery for me. I had gone into the hospital with a protruding stomach and came out without a kidney, and with two wounds and a limp that should have stayed with me for life. But it didn't. I say, "My whole life is a bonus!"

BONUS FROM JONAS
"Don't focus on what you had, focus on what you have, because what you have is enough to get the job done!" A lot of people focus on what they had, but what they had is not going to help them. It is what you have left and implement that can make a positive difference!"

I must say I was glad that the surgery occurred when I was a little boy. Because once I started healing, I didn't pamper myself. I was very tough. I played baseball. I played basketball. I played football. I climbed trees. I was very athletic. I ran myself straight with the help of God. If I had undergone these surgeries when I was an adult, I probably would have pampered myself and worried about injuring myself. That would have led me to have a cautious life instead of living a courageous life. But because I was so young, I did all the things that little boys will do. To live a life of greatness you must be willing to come out of your comfort zone.

BONUS FROM JONAS
"You must be willing to go out on a limb, because after all, that is where the fruit is!"

Because of the severity of the surgery and the doctors' diagnosis of death, I was in the hospital for months. And then finally, I was dismissed from the hospital. However, over a period of several years, I had to be brought back at first on a weekly basis, then every two weeks, then every month, and it got to a point where it became once a year.

I had to travel with my mother from St. Helena Island to Roper Hospital in Charleston, which was 80 miles one way. And we had no transportation. I remember two distinct things about those trips. First, my Auntie Essie (Mrs. Ethel Alston) who baked biscuits just for me. I called them muffins. They were so moist, sweet, and delicious. They just melted in my mouth. And they were just for me. Every time I had to go back to Roper Hospital she would bake them. And I loved them. I was being checked periodically at Roper Hospital to make sure my wound did not turn cancerous.

When I left South Carolina and moved to Rochester, I got a doctor there who monitored me regularly. I was no longer traveling 80 miles to Roper Hospital, now I traveled 969 miles one way from Rochester to St. Helena Island. And every time I would travel home from Rochester to St. Helena Island on vacation, I would get those biscuits/muffins from my Auntie Essie. Even when Auntie Essie got way up in age, and I no longer traveled back and forth to Roper Hospital, she would insist on baking them when she heard that I was home. She continued to bake them until the day that she died. And she would usually make 12 of them at a time. Just for me. Those biscuits/muffins traveled with me from a little boy through adolescence to manhood. And I loved them.

The second fond memory was of Mrs. Helen Galloway who provided the transportation for us to get back and forth from St. Helena Island to Charleston where Roper Hospital was. Mrs. Helen Galloway was a wonderful, kind business-woman, wife, and mother. She owned her own funeral parlor and was very active in the community. She would pick my mother and me up to go to Roper Hospital. And certainly during those days, there was money my mother had to come up with along with assistance from the government to pay Mrs. Galloway. And I remembered her when I grew up and moved to Rochester. When I came home to visit my mother, I would always stop by to visit with Mrs. Galloway. I felt a connection, a level of appreciation and thanksgiving, and a commitment to stop by every time I came home to say to her "thank you."

Because of the giants I have overcome, I am not a survivor. I am an overcomer!

BONUS FROM JONAS
"I have learned that if you hang around with the lame boy or lame girl, or the lame man or the lame woman, you'll learn how to limp!"

Who have you been hanging around with? And how are they affecting your walk? Are they affecting it in a positive way or in a negative way? I was named after Jonah, an Old Testament prophet in the Bible who arose to live to make a dynamic difference in the lives of others. For many years I did not use my first name, Jonas because so many people teased me about my name. There was a stigma associated with the name Jonas that I would have hard luck all of my life.

I used my middle name "Willie" for the first 17 years of my life. Some people had misunderstood the Jonah of the Old Testament.

They thought that the reason the storm came and the ship wouldn't move was because of the name Jonah. But later in life, after I became a Christian, I learned that it wasn't the name that brought bad luck, it was Jonah's behavior. His disobedience to God, which delivered him into the belly of the whale. Later on in life, when anyone teased me about my name, saying it brought "bad luck," I would say, "I am the Jonas who works hard to obey God." Today, I wear my name proudly and I created the phrase "Jonas with the Bonus!"

My father died when I was a little boy. This forced me to learn at an early age the responsibility that I had to work for anything I wanted. So to help out my mother, family, and myself, I used to work on the farm in the summer months to save up money to purchase books, clothing, and materials to use when it was time to go back to school.

My mother is one of my "she-ros" because she was married to my father and all 11 children came as a result of that marriage. She worked hard all of her life from scrubbing floors to working on the farm, from the farm to working in the crab factory, and working hard also to bring up her children with Godly principles. She instilled in us a work ethic, respect of our elders and of others, not to steal, and to get a good education in order to have a better life than she had. She taught me that "manners will take you where money won't," and I've lived long enough to say "I know that's right."

BONUS FROM JONAS
"I'm standing on the shoulders of my ancestors, all that I am or ever hope to be, I owe to God and to my marvelous mother."

Even when the doctors said "no," my mother said, "Yes!" Her "yes!" gave me strength to be the kind of man that I am today. She always will be a great and positive influence in my life. In addition to my mother, the second very special lady in my life is my daughter, Chantieria Joanetta Gadson. After my mother, she has propelled me to become the best man I can be.

BONUS FROM JONAS
"My childhood struggles and triumph over death prepared me tremendously because it is my conviction that if you can overcome death, you can overcome anything! And when you are no longer afraid of dying, then you are prepared for living."

With the challenges of my operations and the stigmas associated with my limp and my name behind me, I encountered a new giant. I was one of 300 students who integrated Beaufort High, a predominantly white high school in Beaufort, South Carolina, in 1970.

In 1964 the Civil Rights Act became law, which prohibited discrimination in public places and in public education all across America. But it was 1970 and Beaufort still practiced the segregation and discrimination that was prevalent in the South at that time. In 1877, the Supreme Court had established that white and black schools were "separate but equal" in the famous Plessey vs. Ferguson case against the State Board of Education of Topeka, Kansas. "Separate but equal" was really separate and unequal. And we experienced that. It meant poor and inferior education for blacks.

It meant torn books, hand-me-down materials, inadequately trained teachers, and substandard education and buildings that did not create effective learning environments. It was designed to make blacks feel inferior and whites feel superior.

In spite of these conditions, I pursued my dreams, my goals, and my aspirations with some level of success. But it wasn't easy. I had to develop a mental attitude to forge ahead in spite of the many challenges I faced. You must be relentless. I developed a positive mindset accompanied with positive action and made up my mind that "where there is a will, there is a way." I was determined to get through. If you can't get through, then you work to go over, if you can't get over, you work to go around, if you can't go around, then you work to go under. But giving up, turning back, or stopping was *not a viable option*. I was pursuing my purpose. And it came at a tremendous price.

BONUS FROM JONAS
"Don't focus on what you can't do, focus on what you can do. And do it! A lot of people give up too early! With just a little bit more 'push' they could achieve their purpose!"

From the first to the eleventh grades, I attended St. Helena Elementary and St. Helena High School, which were predominantly black schools. For 11 years we were accustomed to the community, the culture, and to our school colors— "green and gold." We were the St. Helena Eagles and we were proud of it. We didn't have much but we had one another.

We were a family. We grew up in a culture where we helped one another. What we had we shared. We lived the African proverb that says, "It takes a village to raise a child." All adults, if they saw us doing something wrong, had the right to correct us. And they did. We were poor in material things, but we didn't know that we were poor because of the "sharing and caring" we demonstrated toward one another.

Then, all of a sudden, forced busing came in my senior year and everything changed. We were forced to travel miles away from our community to a completely different environment. School as we knew it was gone.

As a senior, I was bused along with 300 other students from St. Helena High School (Eagles) to Beaufort High, a predominantly white school. This was my first experience with integration. The court ordered busing was forced. We did not want to go to Beaufort High, and some of the parents, some of the teachers and some of the students did not want us to come.

BONUS FROM JONAS
"But I learned in life not to go where the path may lead, but to go where there is no path and leave a trail."

I am a trailblazer and you can be too. I encourage people all over the world not to let your schooling interfere with your education.

I was born during a very dynamic and difficult time in American history. I was born on a plantation in the rural South just as the Civil Rights Movement kicked into gear. I was unaware that this was a critical time in our country. This was a seed that was planted to develop my purpose. I believe as the Old Testament statement says, "That I was chosen for such a time as this."

I always say that I was born so deep in South Carolina until they call it "the LowCountry." Now it is not the end of the world, but you can almost see the end of the world from where I was born.

BONUS FROM JONAS
"It doesn't matter where you were born; it doesn't even matter where you are right now, what does matter is where you are going. So with faith, focus, and fight, you can move from the plantation to becoming the president of your own company, which I have done."

The history of St. Helena Island and my culture is very interesting. More than 40,000 slaves were brought from West Africa, an area known as Angola, and placed on these cluster of islands off the Atlantic Ocean in South Carolina. The ethnicity of these Africans was Mende, Kisi, Malinke, and Bantu. A Creole language, "Gullah," developed from a mixing of the English and African languages. St. Helena Island is one of many such islands known as "the Low Country." Because of the remoteness of the islands, a lot of the African culture and Creole language has remained until today.

And the descendants of African slaves lived on these islands in isolation for many generations, about 300 years, untouched by American culture. The descendants of African slaves brought here have maintained their African culture longer than any slave descendants in America. (1)

In 1971, I graduated from Beaufort High School and moved to Rochester, New York. Having overcome the operations, pain, ridicule, stigmas, discrimination, and forced busing, I came upon a new frontier. Yet another giant. I was a country boy moving from a rural community to my first major city; experiencing not only the drastic change in weather conditions, but in living conditions too. I wasn't used to the close quarters of city living and all of those people. And now, I had to prove myself in getting a job and making a living in my new home.

When I grew up in South Carolina during Christmas we sang "I'm Dreaming of a White Christmas," and I had no concept of what that meant because I had never seen snow. But when I moved to Rochester, that dream turned into a nightmare because there was so much snow, cold, and ice.

I also had to get used to all of the people.

I met more people within a few months there than I had ever met in my first 18 years of living in South Carolina. And they spoke funny.

BONUS FROM JONAS
"When life throws lemons at you, learn the art of how to catch those lemons and make yourself some lemonade and have yourself a spiritual party. However, don't drink all of the lemonade but rather open up a lemonade stand and make yourself some profit."

Another giant. My accent and diction made me stand out when I moved up north to Rochester. I dealt with the challenge by training myself in English and speech.

I realized that the giants weren't going away. In fact, I realized in life that the giants keep on coming.

BONUS FROM JONAS

"Understand that those giants keep on coming and anytime that you decide to pursue greatness you must be prepared to deal with one giant after another. But those giants aren't designed to stop you. They are designed to see how serious you are about your dreams, your goals and your aspirations. As long as you live, you will be dealing with giants if you are committed to making a positive difference and not just a dent."

Immediately, I got involved in a training program to sharpen my skills as I entered a new job market. I entered corporate America and then worked for more than 30 years for Xerox and Eastman Kodak Company, where I developed the expertise, skills, knowledge, and experience to work effectively with people from all around the world.

I had two challenges to overcome in order to become the dynamic and powerful Motivational Speaker that I am today. (1) I came from a different culture and the Gullah language that I spoke was a dialect of the English language. It was like a foreign language and (2) When I learned English, I had been taught incorrectly. So I had to unlearn what I had been taught and begin again.

BONUS FROM JONAS

"I have learned that the first step to the proper education is to unlearn things that I shouldn't have learned in the first place."

Now I am privileged to be able to educate others and share my history and language with you. Early in my speaking career when I began speaking to a diversity of highly educated audiences, I often reminded them that I too, spoke three different languages: "First Southern, second Gullah, and third for the last 10 minutes I've been doing everything I can to speak English."

As I began my career at Eastman Kodak Company, I was a hard worker, very dedicated to my job and I did it effectively but I wasn't growing. There was a paradigm shift, although it wasn't called that at the time. The tension had become very high on the job and the workload was reduced. We were experiencing layoffs, and people were losing their jobs.

The method that management was using to notify individuals that they did not have a job was very insensitive, cold, callous, cruel, and intimidating. This created stress among the workers who had been working for the company for many years.

There was no formal notice, no time to say "goodbye" and no communication on what to expect next. Therefore, all of the line workers feared the day when the boss would tap their shoulder while they were working the assembly line. If this happened, it meant they had just been laid off.

I saw many of my coworkers lose their jobs. I didn't get tapped, but this was my wake-up call. I remember thinking to myself, "If I was to be tapped and laid off would I be prepared to go and get a better job?" I was honest with myself. The answer was "no." From that day on, I decided that I would educate myself, go back to school, take college courses, read, listen to tapes, obtain coaching/tutoring, go to seminars and avail myself of other professional and community resources, and take professional courses to continue to develop myself personally and professionally. This developed my skill set so I would be more marketable in the workplace.

I never turned back from my commitment to pursuing my personal and professional greatness and working on myself because...

BONUS FROM JONAS
"You can always better your best." I believe, as the Bible tells us that "I am more than a conqueror. I am an over-comer." And thanks be to God I have demonstrated this belief since I was a little boy.

Over forty-five years later and I am in "no way tired," and as I said earlier...

BONUS FROM JONAS
"Don't let anyone bury you until after you are dead because you are bigger than that, you are better than that, and the best is still in you. Allow that best to bud, to bloom, and to blossom into a bright and beautiful future!"

I became a lifelong laser learner. I was relentless in pursuing courses, training, reading, and listening to cassettes/CDs. I turned my car into "the university on wheels." I was so hungry for knowledge that I grabbed onto this process and didn't let it go. "We are being bombarded with information but we are starving for knowledge."

Once I became a Christian, I started teaching and was very active in the church and began my Christian ministry. I often spoke, taught and delivered spiritual messages at church, and then from there, expanded my teaching and speaking in the community. I did a lot of hard work continuously with years of relentless preparation.

Once, right after I had delivered a powerful, inspirational message at church and I was greeting the members afterwards, everyone was uplifted and excited. Different people came back and gave me accolades on what a great job I had done. I responded to one of the sisters/members, "I am going back to school and working hard so that I can become a better communicator." She said enthusiastically, "Oh no! You don't have to do anything else. You are good enough."

I didn't reply verbally to her but mentally I had an epiphany. I thought, "This is good enough if this is my destination. It is not. This is just my launching pad." If I had listened to voices like these good-meaning people, I would have never achieved and overcome the different challenges in life for me to become a better human being so that I could impact the world in a positive way..

BONUS FROM JONAS
"Be careful when you sing your own praises because you tend to pitch the tune too high!"

My plan was to motivate people from all different cultures and different socioeconomic levels. And later in my career I achieved this dream. This process of gathering knowledge, being relentless, and developing my gift yielded great success. "It brought me before kings/leaders and great people."

I remember taking a public speaking class at Monroe Community College in Rochester. And it was a diverse class. I think I was the only African-American in the class. And of course, I was still working to develop my communication skills. I gave a speech and some of the students were snickering and poking fun of my speaking. Even the instructor of the class critiqued me harshly. But I overcame their ridicule of my speaking pattern and accent. I said, "Thank you all for the information that you are giving me. You all can laugh if you want, and criticize me. I am here to learn to be a better speaker and I am going to make an A in this class." And I did! This helped propel me to become an even greater motivational speaker.

This motivated me. I turned a negative situation into a positive result and overcame the naysayers. I had the attitude that I wasn't going to let anything or anybody turn me around because I had a positive record of overcoming difficulty. I like what Mr. Whitney Young said, "It is better to be prepared for an opportunity and not have one, than to have an opportunity and not be prepared." This prepared me to begin teaching at schools, colleges, churches, community organizations, and also training at Dale Carnegie after having graduated at the top of my class there. I was invited back twice to help teach and to coach others.

Years later, I joined Toastmasters International, a worldwide speakers' organization with more than 260,000 members, which is known for helping people with their speaking, listening, and leadership skills. I had discovered that what they were teaching was in line with my personal and professional goals and I chose this organization as one of the vehicles that would help me get to my destination and to achieve it with distinction.

As I went through each stage of accomplishment, I created an academic and Olympics metaphor: The CTM (Competent Toastmaster) represented my Associates Degree, my ATM Bronze (Able Toastmaster) my Bachelors Degree, ATM Silver my Master's Degree and DTM (Distinguished Toastmaster), my PhD; my Gold!

Through my active commitment and dedication to the organization, I did exceptional work. I was on the leadership track. As club president I achieved the Distinguished Presidents Award, the Distinguished Area Governor Award, and the club that I was president of we also earned the Distinguished Club recognition. Then, I chartered a new club, and since that club was chartered 10 years ago, it continues to achieve Distinguished Club recognition every year. I competed in and won first place oratorical contests in the area and the division. I taught others how to compete and win oratorical contests as well. And I achieved Distinguished Toastmaster (DTM), this is the highest distinction in Toastmasters International. It takes four to five years to achieve and very few members have achieved this level of accomplishment. Very few members are asked to speak at an International Convention for Toastmasters. I was one of the featured speakers at the Toastmasters International 65th Annual Convention in St. Louis, Missouri. I delivered my signature speech "How To Fly Like An Eagle With Wings Like A Wimp!" to more than 500 people from around the world. My speech remained on the organization's best-seller's list for two consecutive years.

One of my bonuses that I attribute to my success is now on the Toastmasters International worldwide website:

BONUS FROM JONAS
"If you cheat yourself in your preparation, it will show up in your presentation!"

Then, when an opportunity arose at Eastman Kodak Company for the right person to lead a three-year company-wide diversity initiative, endorsed by the president of the company, they didn't need to look far. I was ready and the man chosen for the job. As I always say, "I love speaking so much that I am willing to do it for free. But because I'm so good at it, they are willing to pay me."

I remember the time when I attended a leadership conference in Hershey, Pennsylvania. Of course, Hershey, Pennsylvania is famous for Hershey's chocolate candy. When I lived in Rochester, I received a brochure. I began reading it and learned that it was inviting me to a weekend conference focusing on leadership. I continued to read it and to get even more excited as I read it: Mr. Norman Vincent Peale was one of the sponsors. I read it with enthusiasm and I began envisioning the possibilities.

With further reading I saw it: for Presidents and CEOs *only*. My countenance dropped and I thought to myself, "I want to go but I just know that I will be turned away because it is for Presidents and CEOs only." I studied the brochure for awhile and then I had an epiphany. "Wait a minute." I had just started my own company. "I am the President and CEO of Jonas Gadson Unlimited. My own company." Then I realized, "This is for me!" Right then I decided, "I am going to this conference!"

I paid my money and went to Hershey, Pennsylvania, and stayed in the hotel where the conference was held. It was in a beautiful location and held in a luxurious hotel. Mr. Norman Vincent Peale was the major motivation for me to attend. He was considered to be one of the top motivational speakers and I looked forward to hearing him speak. I had read his books; I was receiving his magazine in the mail, I had listened to him on tape and even watched him on television. But I wanted to meet and hear him in person. After I got there and learned that he wasn't able to be there because he was very ill, I was disappointed.

I had made up my mind a long time ago that I wanted to learn from the Best. However, I adjusted my expectations and then I met his wife, Mrs. Ruth Peale, which was an honor.

BONUS FROM JONAS
"When things go wrong, don't you go wrong with them."

I went up to the very front row, sat down, listened, and took notes. My commitment to me and the mindset I developed was that I would go and always learn from the best and always sit up front because I didn't want to miss anything.

Wherever the speaker was speaking, I positioned myself to be in close proximity because I didn't want to be distracted or miss a word of the message. If I could learn just one new distinction and place it in my "learning arsenal" then it was worth it. I invested in myself and knew I deserved to be there. My focus was to get the knowledge and the skills I needed to develop my personal and professional greatness!

I was so excited that I went around introducing myself to everyone. And after awhile, when other CEOs saw my enthusiasm, they came to greet me and to introduce themselves. I was glad to be there. And this was yet another accomplishment.

BONUS FROM JONAS
I always say, "I'm a victor, not a victim!"

BONUS FROM JONAS
"When life throws bricks at you, learn how to catch those bricks and build yourself a firm foundation so you can stand on the promises and get off the premises!"

These experiences inspired and motivated me to start my own company, Jonas Gadson Unlimited. A Corporate Training Company. A company committed to helping people to develop their personal and professional greatness! These skills helped me to become a motivational speaker, certified trainer, consultant, radio personality, author, and ordained minister to help bring the best out of people while living my purpose with a passion.

I am sharing my knowledge, skills, expertise, and experience with you so you too can be an over-comer. In life, you will have a lot of challenges and obstacles that are placed in your way. But...

BONUS FROM JONAS
"You have to face it in order to erase it!"

In *How To Fly Like An Eagle With Wings Like A Wimp!* you will get "true, tried, and tested techniques" that will help you "live your purpose with a passion."

On Becoming an Eagle

A story was told about a little eagle in an egg that was accidentally placed in a chicken's nest with other eggs. And the mother hen sat on all of the eggs. When it was time for the eggs to hatch, of course, all of the chickadees looked just like their mother, the mother hen. However, there was also a strange looking bird, the eaglet. As time went on, the chickadees grew up to be chickens, but the eaglet now became a full-grown eagle. And one day he decided to look around, and he noticed that he did not look like the mother chicken nor did he look like any of the other chickens. But he worked diligently to act, to behave, to scratch, and to eat like his brothers and sisters (siblings).

One day, when he was out in the yard, he looked up and suddenly saw a strange bird. He kept looking and looking and said, "Hmmm, that bird looks just like me. But why can't I fly like that big bird in the sky?" He quickly dismissed that sighting and forgot about that big flying bird and went on back to scratching, acting, and pretending to be a chicken. One day, a naturalist came by and noticed an eagle amongst the chickens. He said to the farmer, "That's an eagle, but he's acting like a chicken." The farmer said, "Well, he doesn't know that he is an eagle, he thinks that he is a chicken." The naturalist said to the farmer, "Can I teach him how to be an eagle and how to fly?" And the farmer said, "Go ahead, but it's not going to do any good, he thinks that he is a chicken."

The next day, the naturalist came, caught the eagle and threw it up in the air. And of course, the eagle flew a little, looked down, saw the chickens and went back down, behaving like one of them.

And the next day, the naturalist came back and he decided this time to take the eagle on top of the barn and he said to the eagle, "You are an eagle, you are supposed to fly. You are not a chicken."

So he threw the eagle into the air from the barn, and of course, the eagle flew just a little and he looked down and he saw the chickens and he went on back down, continuing to act like a chicken.

But on the third day, the naturalist came back and was determined to help this eagle to fly and to be the great bird that he was created to be. So he took the eagle, took him off of the farm and up into the mountains and he climbed way above all the trees away from the eagle's normal environment with the chickens and he said, "You are an eagle, so go ahead, go ahead and fly." Again he threw the eagle up into the air. But this time as the eagle began to fly with his wings outstretched he began to look down once again to the ground. Fortunately, this time he did not see the chickens and on that day he learned to fly far above his environment. And it was then that he realized that he was an eagle and not a chicken.

Many times we as individuals (humans) go around in life scratching, acting like we are chickens, when really we were designed to fly, not to fall; we were designed to climb, not to crawl; we were designed to soar, not to sink. This book is designed to challenge you "to take a chance, take charge, and to take control of your life" and to help you to realize that regardless of the challenges that you went through in the past; regardless of the challenges that you are going through in the present, and regardless of the challenge that you predict for the future, I am helping you to realize that you can fly again.

You can fly above mediocrity. You can fly above your environment. You can fly above your education. You can fly above alcoholism. You can fly above drugs. You can fly above depression and other addictions. You can fly above your own limitations, above the expectations of others. Fly above "I can't do it!"

BONUS FROM JONAS
**"When we look at what others are doing
we get impressed. When we look at what
we are doing or think we can't do, we get depressed.
When we look up and depend on God for our greatness
We are continually blessed!"**

You can develop the greatness that is within you. You can fly like the eagle that you were "designed and destined to be." I wrote this book to help you to re-ignite the eagle spirit that is in you!

What Kind of Bird Are You?

BONUS FROM JONAS
The Greatest Enemy to Greatness
is not that we aim too high and miss,
it's that we aim too low and hit!
What kind of bird are you?

There are 9,000 species of birds in the world. All birds have their unique characteristics and there are many different special qualities of human beings. There is a direct correlation between the behavior of birds and the behavior of humans. I am using these birds including eagles as metaphors to demonstrate the human and bird similarities as well as differences.

Chicken

The chicken can only lift up a little off of the ground. When it tries to fly there is a lot of activity but it does not accomplish anything. The flight is bumpy, uncertain and short-lived. A whole lot of energy is spent, a lot of flapping occurs, but it isn't going anywhere in flight. It is always scratching around looking for leftovers. It has an "entitlement" mentality. It is a follower and not a leader. In America there are 365 ways to cook a chicken. It is the most eaten bird in America. If you aren't making plans for your life, someone else is. And you will be cooked and eaten.

Duck

It is always quacking in disagreement with someone else's idea, dream, goals and aspirations. It is always complaining, criticizing, and condemning but never offers any positive solutions. It is a reluctant follower. It is never satisfied. It is always quacking.

It is always complaining and it makes a disgruntled follower. If it leads, it only leads in quacking.

Peacock

This bird is proud, colorful, flamboyant and must be the center of attention. But it has no substance. It always focuses on "me" and we never hear it speak about "we." It is prideful, feels as if it is "A bag of chips and all that." It dances to the beat of its own drum. It is not interested in leading... only in being the center of attention.

It wants to be the bridegroom or bride in every wedding but it doesn't want to be married. It wants to be the corpse in every funeral but it doesn't want to die.

Turkey

Gobble! Gobble! Gobble! "Birds of a feather flock together." This bird always travels in groups, but that still doesn't protect it from being killed and eaten. It is not willing to stand alone. It is a loser. Waiting for someone else to direct its actions and live for it. This means that every Thanksgiving it ends up as the main course on someone's dining table. It lacks control of its life and is willing to turn it over to others. Once a year in America, around Thanksgiving, the U.S. president pardons one turkey while millions of other turkeys are on dinner tables waiting to be eaten. Gobbling and being led or influenced by the majority of turkeys doesn't lead to liberation. It leads to the end of your life.

Turkeys are fed and fattened for someone else's consumption (purpose).

Parakeet

This bird is busy duplicating others and never becomes what it is designed to be. It lives the "Polly want a cracker" mentality. It mimics others and I call it the "great pretender." It is being a copy of others instead of being an original of itself. It is always in identity crisis. Any way that the wind blows is okay with the parakeet. It has a "take a poll" mentality. It doesn't think for itself because that takes hard work.

Ostrich

There is an African ostrich, a special breed of ostrich that grows to weigh as much as 300 pounds and is the fastest running bird on earth. It can run at top speeds of 42 mph and can maintain 31 mph running as long as 15 to 20 minutes. However, when it can no longer run from life, it sticks its head in the sand. It thinks that it is safe with its head in the sand while the world is kicking its butt. It believes that "ignorance is bliss."

It believes, "What I don't know can't hurt me." In reality, what it doesn't know is going to kill it. It hollers, "I want to be free!" Yet it refuses to acknowledge that freedom comes with responsibility and accountability. It thinks, "If I can't see it, then I surely am not responsible to be it."

Vulture

This bird preys on the failure of others. It is a natural predator. The odor given off by a dead or dying animal has a stench that is repulsive to our nostrils; however, this smell is an aroma of sweet perfume to the buzzard/vulture. It lives off the remains of the dead...It waits patiently for the death of its prey. It is a personality that waits for you to give up on your dreams, goals and aspirations so it can say, "I told you so." It is a taker, not a giver. "I got you." It is a leader but a leader of deadly destruction.

Sparrow

In the bird world there are millions of sparrows. Sparrows fly low to the ground and never venture far from home. Sparrows stay in their comfort zone and play it safe. They like familiarity. But familiarity breeds complacency. Sparrows aim low and stay low.

Eagle

Each one of us was designed to be an eagle. We were designed to fly, not to fall; to climb, not to crawl; to soar, not to sink... Perhaps all of us at some time in our lives encountered situations where we adopted the thinking, behavior and personality of one or some of the birds described above. This determines the destination of each bird and of every human being. We had wings that didn't allow us to fly. What kind of behaviors are you exhibiting? Of all the birds we have named, you were compared to an eagle. This book is written and dedicated to you to give you your wings back, help you tap into your eagle potential, and re-ignite the eagle spirit that was placed in you.

How To Fly Like An Eagle With Wings Like A Wimp! is designed to feed the eagle spirit in you so you too can fly again.

A Tribute to My Marvelous Mother

Mrs. Eliza Mary Gadson

I dedicate this book, *How To Fly Like An Eagle With Wings Like A Wimp!*, to my marvelous mother, Mrs. Eliza Mary Gadson.

I was blessed to have the greatest mother who ever lived! We were very close. All of the older people used to tell me that I look exactly like my mother! When I began this book a number of years ago, my mother was very much a part and an inspiration to me! I even gathered some additional information and input from her. Certainly my goals and aspirations were that we would celebrate together at the completion of my book! However, over the years, my mother's health continued to decline, and for more than 33 years, I commuted back and forth from Rochester, New York, to St. Helena Island, South Carolina, to spend quantity and quality time with my mother. We would always have a great time together, visiting the elderly people, and singing and praying for them. She was always "other focused"!

In 2005 it became necessary, because of her health, for me to relocate from Rochester to St. Helena Island to help take care of my marvelous mother. She took care of me when I couldn't take care of myself. So I developed the mindset that my mother wasn't going to be placed in an "old folks home" because she never put me in the "young folks home."

I always believed in giving my mother her flowers while she was living so she could see them and smell them. My mother also had a Great sense of humor! And a beautiful smile! I remember numerous times in the three and a half years back and forth to the doctors and to the hospital...I remember while I talked with her at the bedside. I started teasing her. I said, "I know that you are glad that you stuck by my side.... Out of 11 children, I was your sickest child and wasn't expected to live. Who would have thought that I would be the child who would take care of you now! Aren't you glad that you took care of me?" She would just laugh.

My mother was a sharp dresser! She loved for me to bring things from Rochester for her. I remember for many years I would come home and take her shopping to Savannah, Georgia. This time I came home and I took her to her favorite dress store in Savannah. She was just smiling and so happy. On this occasion, she tried on five different dresses and she fell in love with all five of them. I asked, "Which one do you love the best?" She said, "It's a hard decision; I love all of them!"

I said, "I'll just purchase them all!" And she lit up and was so radiant. Her look, her joy, her happiness, really lifted my spirits.

When we got back to her house sometimes I would take a nap or I would have gone to bed for the night. When I awoke, I would overhear her talking on the telephone to her friends early in the morning. She was bragging on me and the brand new dresses and outfits that I bought her. The joy and excitement that she expressed made me feel so good because she deserved it! She had sacrificed so much over the years for all of her children.

She also was a very good cook. And of course I learned a lot from her. But there's one special dish that I love and although I worked very hard to make it the way my mother did, I could never get it like hers. So when I came home from Rochester I always wanted my mother to cook red rice for me. I could eat a whole pot full by myself. Well, I never did get that red rice right. But it is etched in my subconscious mind and in my taste buds. Every time I have a desire for some, I go back down memory lane and envision my mother cooking that red rice just for me!

In addition to teaching me how to cook she taught me many life lessons. Here are a few of the lessons that I learned from my marvelous Mother! She taught me manners and respect. My mother always said to me, "Boy, manners will take you where money won't."And I've lived long enough to say, "I know that's right!"

Another valuable lesson she taught me was not to steal. If someone was trying to hurt me or take advantage of me and I fought to defend myself and got arrested she would come down to the jail to get me out provided I was trying to protect myself. However, if I was arrested because of stealing, she would not come to get me. So consequently, I was never arrested for stealing. She taught me the difference between right and wrong. She taught me that she was not going to support me for doing the wrong thing.

Another lesson that my mother taught me was the value of hard work and earning money honestly. She demonstrated determination and faith in God and put our needs ahead of hers. When we worked on the farm during the summer, the monies were given to my mother to help with our school-books, clothing, shoes, and our family needs. Being a widow, my mother worked on the farm, scrubbed other people's floors, and worked in the Lunkin Crab Factory to make ends meet. Then she came home and did the daily cooking and cleaning for our large family. She had a strong character and could not be moved when she put her mind to something. She accomplished great things with this mindset. And I learned this quality from her.

I remember working with my brother Abraham on the farm, and we were in great demand as a team. The farmers were happy because they knew that we were hard workers! I worked so hard one day that I made $35 in one day! That was unheard of! When I got home I never even thought about keeping some of the money back.

It never entered into my mind! I gave the entire $35 to my mother. I was so excited when my mother gave me 50¢ back! During those days you could get a 16-ounce Dixie Cola soda, a sweet roll, and a quarter's worth of lunch meat. For me I thought, "It doesn't get any better than this!" The values I learned from my mother I still live by today.

My mother was the first person who taught me what "motivation" was all about.

She was motivated to give us a better life! She stuck by me and this makes me honor her as a marvelous mother. My mother came up on the rough side of the mountain but that didn't stop her from climbing. I have been extremely blessed!

And we need these kind of committed mothers today!

On Thursday, February 21, 2008, I remember so vividly getting up that morning and checking my mother's blood sugar, preparing breakfast for her, and making sure she was bathed and helping her to get dressed for another challenging but great day. And all of a sudden—this had happened numerous times over the last three and a half years—she had another attack! I called 911 as I had done many times before. They came. She had stopped breathing. Her heart had stopped and they were working on her in her bedroom. And it seemed as if my heart had stopped too.

One of the medical assistants who came in the ambulance said they thought she had a do-not-resuscitate request! I said, "No. Keep working on her!" So they kept working on her and they took her out to the ambulance to rush her once more to Beaufort Memorial Hospital. I ran out and yelled, "Don't you stop working on her! Do whatever it takes to revive my mother!" I jumped in my car and drove to Beaufort Memorial Hospital.

Only this time was different than all the other times. When I got there, I wasn't able to go into the ER as I had done in the past. They put me in another room and asked if there was anything they could do for me. It was one of the loneliest times in my life. A doctor came in and said to me, "Mr. Gadson, we did all that we could, but your mother has passed away." I was shocked! I was devastated! I was numb! And I also was lost! How am I going to make it without my marvelous mother?

I requested that they take me to where my mother was. Talk about the longest, loneliest walk I ever faced. There she was, motionless, not breathing. My mother, who gave me life, who believed in me, who accepted me for who I was. Just lying there. I couldn't believe it.

I went over to her, touched her, and burst out crying like I never cried before. I spent about an hour there, just me and my mother. I stayed there as long as I could until they came and told me that they had to move my mother's body and take it to the morgue because someone else needed to use this room. I had never been in a room with someone who had just died. Especially my mother. But after crying for a long period of time and holding my mother's hand and touching her, I discovered to my surprise, that I learned there was a natural process of living. And this was dying. And of course, it was a tough grieving process.

On Thursday, February 21, 2008, when I left Beaufort Memorial Hospital this time, it was without my marvelous mother. That's when I relied even more on my faith. One of the verses in the Bible that helped me was Psalms 27:10. It says, "When your mother and father forsake you, then the Lord will take you up." In fact, it's been over two years since my marvelous mother passed away. And I am still feeling the void. What I have also learned when you can't sleep at night because of the loss of a loved one...

BONUS FROM JONAS
"Don't stay up all night counting the sheep. Turn and talk to the Shepherd. He will bring you through."

I delivered my mother's eulogy at her funeral on Thursday February 28, 2008, for which I was grateful. But it was the most difficult thing that I have ever done.

In 2000, when I came home to St. Helena Island from Rochester, New York, for the funeral of my baby brother Abraham Gadson, my mother sat me down and told me what her wishes were when she died. This is what she wanted me to do. She told me what outfit she wanted to be buried in, instructed me to take it to the cleaners and make sure it was in "tip-top" shape. Then, she told me what little monies she had.

She told me what her last will and testament was. She also told me, "Son, I don't want to be buried back in those old woods." She told me specifically what cemetery she wanted to be buried in: St. Helena Memorial Garden. I had never heard of the cemetery. As she was talking to me, I felt very uncomfortable, wondering internally, "Mother, why are you telling me this? I probably will die before you."

Then she continued and said, "I know you are going to do my eulogy. And I want you also to make sure that my pastor [of her church] gets to say a few words. Even in her death, she was still teaching me and strengthening me to be a better man. She planned it in such a way by telling me that I will do the eulogy, which I never ever dreamt of doing in a thousand years, because I never imagined life without my marvelous mother.

But I did do the eulogy. Yes! It took every part of my being and a lot of help from God. But she helped me to become even a better man, to do something as tough as that! I followed her wishes completely. Individuals at the funeral were talking about how beautiful she looked in the coffin. They complimented me.

I responded, "My mother planned everything before she died." I never knew the cemetery. But I found it and purchased a plot there. My mother was still teaching me. Even in her death. She was teaching me lessons that I would have never learned without her. All those in attendance were encouraged and edified by my words. She has left a large emptiness that only God can fill and I am grateful for the kind of relationship that I was privileged to have with my mother.

I am a stronger man because of Mrs. Eliza Mary Gadson!

Our mother's favorite Bible verse was "I will lift up mine eyes unto the hills, from whence cometh my help. My help cometh from the Lord, which made heaven and earth" (Psalms 121: 1–2). Everything that I am or ever hope to be, I owe it all to God and to my marvelous mother.

Special Dedication to Family and Friends

Living and Leaving a Legacy of Greatness!

I dedicate this book to my dynamic daughter, Miss Chantieria Joanetta Gadson. Chantieria, I am very proud of you and I love you very much!

Special thanks to my Aunt Louise Smalls for your help, support, and love, and the examples that you have demonstrated to my mother, to me, and to the Gadson family. For you, I am eternally grateful.

Auntie Gal. Ms. Mary Owens, you have been a very present light in my life. I am eternally grateful for you!

Dedication to and in loving memory of:

Mrs. Eliza Mary Gadson, my mother
Lillian Gadson-Holmes
Emily Gadson
Joseph Gadson
Abraham Gadson
"Auntie Essie" Ms. Ethel Alston
Eva Alston
Mrs. Margaret McClary
Minister Edgar D. Brown and wife Candice
Mrs. Helen Galloway

Special Thanks To:
Mr. Cecil McClary Sr. and Family
Mrs. Mary McClary Hill
Mr. Carl King

And loving thanks to all of those who have made a positive impact in my life: To all of those whom I have spoken to, encouraged and worked with; to those who have helped me with my book and bringing it to fruition. I appreciate you tremendously and I Thank You!

CHAPTER ONE

The Characteristics of the Eagle

THE EAGLE IS UNIQUE. HE IS THE MOST POWERFUL bird in the sky: He is the king of the air. There are specific characteristics that make the eagle who he is. He symbolizes freedom, strength, and courage. Studying the eagle will give you a small glimpse of the nature and the greatness of God. The eagle has keen vision and focus: Its eyesight is five to six times sharper than that of a human being. It has been said that the eagle has the ability to see at least 7 miles in any direction. The eyesight of an eagle is sharp and he uses three sets of lenses. He uses his panoramic lens to scan the horizon from a distance; he uses his zoom-in lens to bring objects that are far away closer so that he can better examine them to decide if they are worth pursuing. He uses his protective lens when he looks directly into the sun so that his eyesight is not damaged. This is something no other bird, animal, or human can do.

The eagle has the discipline of focus and does not allow himself to be deterred by any distractions. Because of this, he gets a larger vision of his prey.

The eagle is a finicky eater. The eagle doesn't put any dead or already killed animal into his mouth unless he is in captivity.

He eats salmon and fish and animals that he has hunted himself, and has decided that this is what he wants to eat today.

And no substitute will do. He knows what he wants and he isn't satisfied for anything less. If today he wants a rabbit, a squirrel will not do. And he will do whatever it takes to get the rabbit. If the rabbit hides from the eagle and goes into a hole, the eagle gets a perch out of sight and waits patiently and quietly until the rabbit comes out. Then the eagle swoops down and gets the rabbit. He demonstrates the stamina to be patient and wait while he works. What is it that you want today? And are you willing to work while you wait to get what you want?

The eagle develops strong muscles in order to lift up his prey. Just as the eagle uses his muscles to lift up his prey, we must use our muscles to lift ourselves up. If we don't develop and use the muscles we have then those muscles will atrophy. "If you don't use it, you'll lose it." If we don't pursue our purpose to become the eagle that we were destined to be, then we die never having reached our full potential. Are you willing to allow that to happen? What are you using your muscles to lift?

The eagle has the ability to fly high and fly fast. His wing capacity can be 16 feet in diameter when both wings are extended. It has been said that the eagle has the ability to fly to speeds of up to 200 miles per hour. Faster than any other bird. He can fly as high as 10,000 feet in the air. Something no other bird can do.

The eagle accepts responsibility and knows how to take care of himself and prepare for life's upcoming challenges. When a storm is approaching, an eagle can see up to 7 miles in the distance. Then he gets busy. He flies upward and then swoops straight down into the water at high speeds to get all of the debris off of his body.

He uses his skills and talents with wisdom, and calculates and discerns how fast to fly. It has been said that the eagle has the capability to fly up to 200 miles per hour, but he only uses it when he needs it. Then, he examines every feather and coats it with a special kind of solution that God gave him, which protects the feathers.

He plucks out any and all old and damaged feathers.

And then, he flies into the storm in a circular manner. As he flies directly into the storm in a circular way, he uses the wind as an updraft. He is going higher and higher and pretty soon he is flying above the storm. Sometimes in life the reason why we are being devastated by the storms is that we are flying too low. (Or we try to outrun the storm, or we succumb to the storm.) We never think that there is another option. You can learn how to fly above the storm. You must be willing to do what it takes to go to another altitude. Higher than where we have ever been before. We can move to a new altitude and fly above the storm. Just like the eagle, if we want to fly higher, we must prepare ourselves like the eagle does, and accept responsibility for where we are, be willing to do what it takes, so that we too are able to fly above our storms.

BONUS FROM JONAS
"The greatest enemy to greatness is not that we aim too high and miss, its that we aim too low and hit!"

The eagle welcomes the storm. He sees it as a blessing, not a blister. He uses the storm to guarantee his victory. In life you get what you prepare for. Opportunity doesn't knock, it resides in you. And it resides in me.

From Victim to Victor to Gain the Victory

The storm has the potential to turn the eagle into a victim, but the eagle doesn't allow this. You can be victim to the storms of life or you can do as the eagle does and become a Victor. Are you going to be a victim or are you going to be a victor?

The choice is yours. Many times we become volunteer victims. This book is written to encourage you to choose to be a victor and give you the "education, inspiration, and motivation" necessary to gain your victory. The eagle uses the storm to gain his victory.

BONUS FROM JONAS
"If you don't handle your storms properly, your storms will handle you."

We have a choice. When we handle our storm, we refuse to be a victim. We use the storm to become a victor so that we can gain our victory. It starts with our perception. Your storm can be a blessing but most of us view it as a blister. The eagle uses his lenses to make sure his perception is correct. He uses these lenses to get the right perception. If his perception is off then the outcome or results will be off.

BONUS FROM JONAS
"In order to be you must see! Whatever you see... is what you will be. If you want to be more you must first see more!"

The eagle uses his zoom in lens to make sure that his perception is right to back up what he first saw with his panoramic lens. In the story of the *Titanic*, the ship's captain, Commodore Edward J. Smith's judgment and perception were off.

His vision was incorrect. He might have seen 10 percent of the iceberg. What he didn't see was the other 90 percent, which was a massive iceberg underwater. What they saw didn't bring the *Titanic* down. It was what they didn't see. "The unsinkable *Titanic*" created an attitude that caused the captain not to see the obvious.

BONUS FROM JONAS
"When your belief system has been affected, it distorts your perception!"

He didn't check his perception and as a consequence 1,523 people lost their lives. (2) A lot of times our perception is off. How do you view your world? Your surroundings? How do you view you?

I know the true me and you know the true you. Sometimes we portray a false representation of who we are. This book is designed to help you reveal the true you. We are taught to be the great pretenders. I don't show you who I really am because if I do, you may not like me. And I don't want to be rejected. So you tell me what you want me to be and I'll pretend to be it. Put me on something green, I'll be green; put me on something brown, I'll be brown; put me on something gray, I'll become gray.

BONUS FROM JONAS
"God made you an original;
don't you dare die a cheap copy."

On the other hand, the eagle is a great contender. The eagle has the power; he has the strength; and he has confidence. He doesn't pretend to be any other bird.

The eagle knows he is unique and he is the king of the air. You don't have to live your life appeasing others. You are biologically unique; you are divinely designed. When you are divinely designed you are destined for greatness.

Are you being a great pretender or are you being a great contender?

The eagle is one of the only birds that does not fly south when the winter approaches. And when a storm comes, he flies directly into it and uses it to empower him. He insulates himself. He has prepared for the storm and uses it to his benefit. Are you prepared for the storms of life?

BONUS FROM JONAS
"You don't want to approach the storms of life
casually because if you do you run the risk of
ending up a casualty."

BONUS FROM JONAS
"Don't run to God telling Him how big
your storm is. Rather run to your storm
and remind it how big God is!"

The eagle uses the wind as an updraft and the storm becomes "the wind beneath his wings." When the eagle uses the storm as an updraft, he uses the storm to empower him—to gain its power— using its strength to his benefit. The storm has the potential to turn him into a victim, but he uses the storm so he can gain the victory.

BONUS FROM JONAS
"You will either die in the bleachers as a spectator or
you will die on the field as a participant! I am here to
call you out as a participant into the game of life! It's
your time to fly. It's 'Now-O'Clock'!"

Don't rust out in the bleachers but wear out on the field as a participant.

On February 2, 2007, a devastating tornado hit Lady Lake County in central Florida, early in the morning and destroyed a lot of property and 19 people lost their lives. (3) They showed a church building on national television. The preacher indicated how surprised he was that the church collapsed. The church had been built to withstand a storm with 150 mph winds. The tornado that hit was only 110 mph, and it destroyed the church building completely.

As the reporters were zooming their cameras in on the debris, they captured a church song book opened to this song: "I Surrender All to Thee!" If a lifeless building has enough submission, what about you and what about me? If you prepare yourself for the storms in life, you too can gain your victory. To try to outrun a storm is not a viable strategy.

BONUS FROM JONAS
"If God brings you to it, He has the power to bring you through it!"

When I was living in Rochester, I had to learn the importance of winterizing my home and insulating my pipes to prepare for the harsh winters. This is what this book is designed to do. To help you prepare. To winterize your life.

Many times as human beings we live in isolation instead of taking the necessary steps to prepare ourselves to properly insulate our lives against the predators of life. What if we take the time to insulate our goals, our dreams, and our aspirations?

BONUS FROM JONAS
"Many of us are called but most of us are frozen!"

Why? Because we did not take the initiative to insulate ourselves. We didn't prepare ourselves. So we left ourselves exposed. We are living a life of default versus living a life of favor. The future belongs to those who prepare for it. And some people are blaming the recession for their failures.

BONUS FROM JONAS
"Recession is my time for possession!"

When the eagle gets old, it cannot fly at the same speed; its eyes are not as keen and it is not as strong as it used to be. And because of this, other birds decide to gang up on the eagle to overtake him. But he still has his wisdom and he still can fly higher than all of the other birds. When the other birds come to gang up on him and get on his back to bring him down, if the altitude doesn't take them off, the eagle takes them to the sun and the sun burns them off.

When there comes a time in our lives when we are not as strong as we used to be, not as vigilant, and when we can't move as fast...When human predators work to attack and take advantage of us to destroy us, we need to use our wisdom and to take them to the Son. The Son will help us. "If the Son therefore shall make you free, you are free indeed" (St. John 8:36).

If you want to catch the eagle, you must catch him one eagle at a time. He is an independent, solitary bird. "Birds of a feather flock together" does *not* apply to the eagle.

When it comes to his family, he is also an interdependent bird. As we said earlier, eagles are finicky eaters. This is the same principle they use in selecting a mate. When it comes to selecting a mate eagles are also very finicky. A female eagle has a unique way of selecting her mate. She will pick up a twig and fly high into the air and drop it. Several male eagles will fly beneath her and work diligently to catch that twig. This test continues until one of the male eagles catches the twig three times. That eagle is selected by the female to be her mate.

The female is testing the male for his ability to catch the young eaglets as they are directed out of the nest to learn how to fly. When it is time for the young eaglet to fly on its own, the mother eagle pushes her young out of the nest. Then she catches them and carries the young eaglets on her back, up high into the air, and shakes them off.

It is the responsibility of the father eagle to swoop down and catch the young eaglets until they learn to fly on their own. The female eagle is testing the male for his responsibility and holds him accountable for catching the eaglets.

She has confidence in this male eagle that he has the ability, the dedication, and the commitment and she believes she can depend on him because he demonstrated it when he caught the twig. She also believes that the male eagle doesn't mind being held accountable and responsible. When she shakes one eaglet at a time off her back/wings at a high altitude, the expectation is that the eaglet will stick out its wings and fly. If the eaglet does not, the father eagle will be able to swoop down and catch each one consistently and not allow it to crash, get damaged, injured, or even worse—killed.

The father eagle continues to demonstrate responsibility and accountability as he loves, protects, and provides for his family. Eagles work together to realize their purpose as a family. When the eaglet egg is being incubated, the mother and father eagles demonstrate the importance of working together to protect their eaglets. They each take turns in sitting on the eaglet eggs for 35 days to hatch them. This is securing and protecting the future of their family. It is paramount for us as human beings to be independent *and* interdependent working together as a family in harmony to secure the future for our children.

On July 4, 2007, we in the United States had the privilege and honor to celebrate the comeback of the eagle. (4) The eagle is a symbol of freedom in America, and because of man's poor choices, it was in danger of extinction 50 years ago in 1960. Today, the eagle has come back and is no longer in danger of extinction. There are 10,000 breeding pairs of bald eagles in America today.

There are 310 million people living in America today. (5) The total population of America is also being threatened: People are not living to their full potential. They don't realize that they are eagles and are living beneath their privileges.

We as humans have been styled as the eagle. It is time for us to make a comeback and live our lives as we were designed. Come back to our dreams, our goals, and our aspirations. Come back to our Creator and be all that He designed and destined us to be.

Eagles symbolize freedom, strength, and courage. This book is about developing the courage to use your strength which is already in you and use the freedom to fly to higher heights than you've ever flown before.

God has a plan for Your Life. "Plans to prosper you... plans to give you hope and a future" (Jeremiah 29:11).

BONUS FROM JONAS
"My future is so bright I need to wear sunglasses!"

"But they that wait upon the Lord shall renew their strength; they shall mount up with wings as eagles; they shall run and not be weary; and they shall walk, and not faint" (Isaiah 40:31).

"Develop Patience"

As the scripture says, "They that wait upon the Lord..." When you talk about waiting on the Lord it is not talking about a passive sitting around or waiting for someone to ride in on a white horse to rescue you out of mediocrity. This wait is talking about working as you wait. Activity.

"Wait Upon the Lord"

Whatever your challenge is, whatever your hurts, habits, and hang-ups are, you can put it down upon the Lord. He said, "I will never leave thee neither foresake thee." In fact He said, "I will help you."

"Shall Renew"

This book is designed and written to renew you. To re-mind you who you are and whose you are. You are divinely designed and destined to be the eagle that you were created to be.

"The Strength"

He promised to give you the strength that you need to live the purpose that He has created you for. They shall mount up with wings like an eagle: This is your time. "You have been chosen for such a time as this." Aren't you tired of mounting down? This book is about mounting you UP. Empowering You.

Releasing the power that has been lying dormant in you. It is time to let it out. To lose you and the greatness that is within you. To help you learn how to fly again. You are an eagle.

"And They Shall Run"

It's time to run. It is time to lay aside every weight that will impede your progress, keeping you from reaching your divine destination. You are in a race. And its time to run.

"And Not Be Weary"

Don't give up. I know that you might be going through some difficult times right now. Maybe you've lost your job, maybe you've lost your loved one, maybe you are dealing with the deadly impact and numbing effect of divorce. But remember, the operable word here is that you are "going" through. And since you are going through, don't meander. Hurry up and come on through. And this book is written not only to help you go through but to help you grow through. So don't give up.

"And, They Shall Walk..."

...not waller, not crawl, not jump, not skip, not run, But walk.

"And Not Faint."

Fainting is not a healthy option. It is not a strategy for success. It is a strategy that leads to death. This is not the time to faint or to fall out. Some people are volunteering to have the tranquilizer injected into their bodies that will cause them to fall out or go to sleep. I am here to wake you out of your sleep; from using this method to keep you unconscious and in your comfort zone. I am here to make you conscious. To pull you out of your comfort zone and to awaken the greatness that is within You. In difficult times, when you are hit from the blind side and you are going to fall, always strive to fall forward, that puts you closer to your divine destination. It is time to take action.

BONUS FROM JONAS
"You might have heard that good things come to those who wait, but it is usually the things leftover from those who hustle."

It is your time to learn how to fly again. Don't wait. Congratulations on your wise decision to invest in the most important person on the planet *you.*

Welcome to

How To Fly Like An Eagle With Wings Like A Wimp!

Chapter Two

Eyesight:
Vision, Value, Voice

E-Eyesight

As stated in Chapter One the eagle has the ability to see approximately 7 miles at a time. Its eyesight is so powerful, sharp and keen that it zooms right in on its subject, its prey. The eagle's eyesight is five to six times sharper and more powerful than the human's sight and it is very focused. It is important as human beings for us to stay focused as well because life is full of distractions. There is a direct correlation between the eagle and humans. It is essential that both humans and the eagle use the discipline of focus to achieve their purpose. It is important that you stay focused and get a larger vision of yourself. It has been said that the eyes are the windows to the soul. When you look through your eyes, what is it that you see for yourself?

BONUS FROM JONAS
"Eyesight is what you see;
your vision is what you can be!"

Here are some additional questions that you must ask and answer for yourself before you move on. Who are you? Where are you now? Where you are going?

How do you plan to get there? When you have arrived, will you know? What are you going to do once you have arrived? It is important that you tap into your potential. Your Personal Power. Your Uniqueness and Your Greatness.

The first thing you need to do is get a larger vision of yourself. See yourself differently: as a doctor, lawyer, or teacher; owning your own business; writing your book; singing that song; painting that portrait; going back to school and completing your high school diploma, or getting your G.E.D.; taking online courses to strengthen your skills. Going back to college and getting your degree: Associates, Bachelors, Masters, or Ph.D. What is it for you? I don't know. Yet, one thing I do know is that you have to first "see it to be it."

BONUS FROM JONAS
"If we have high expectations but low preparation that will lead to frustration and desperation!"

As I said earlier...

BONUS FROM JONAS
"What you see is what you are going to be. If you want to be more, you must first see more."

And just like the eagle, you must stay focused, whatever your dreams, goals and aspirations are. And, we will talk more about that in future chapters. But for now...

BONUS FROM JONAS
"Whatever you focus on the longest will become the strongest."

What specifically are you focusing on? What is it that you want? Certainly, in order to achieve it, it requires two Ws: work and worth.

First, is hard *work*. You have to be willing to burn the midnight oil. You have to sacrifice. Be willing to do whatever it takes as long as it is positive and purposeful.

It may require you to go back to school, go to more seminars, read more positive books, take more classes, listen to more CDs, and watch more DVDs, get a mentor or a coach, pay more attention to positive sermons, and listen to lyrics that will build your spirit. You have to build around yourself positive, powerful and purposeful people who are willing to help you. You cannot do it alone.

BONUS FROM JONAS
"Even the Lone Ranger had Tonto."

The second W is *worth*. You must believe that you are worth it! And, once you believe and know that you are worth it, you will do the work. That will cause you to pursue your dreams with tenacity. You cannot rise any higher than where you see yourself.

That's why it is critical that we work on our self-image and our self-worth, and cultivate healthy self-esteem. Because if our self-worth and our self-image are distorted, it will impact our self-esteem in a negative way. If you don't get to the core of your self-worth, you will live a mediocre life rather than a life of significance.

BONUS FROM JONAS
"If you cheat yourself in your preparation, it will show up in your presentation!"

You must understand, however, that I am not talking about selfishness. I am talking about what is essential. It is critical that you work on you because you are worth it. Just like the eagle uses his zoom in lens to zoom in on his prey, you must use your eyesight to zoom in on yourself to do a self-assessment of your worth. Your worth is not in things. Your worth is in you.

BONUS FROM JONAS
"Your thoughts affect your talk and your talk affects your walk! If you want a different walk, you *must* work on developing positive thoughts!"

Your subconscious mind cannot differentiate between truth and error; it is committed to make sure that you are right. If you believe you can't achieve greatness, then your subconscious mind will bring up data of your past failures to reassure you that you will fail again. However, if you believe that you can achieve greatness, then your subconscious mind along with you works to bring up data of your past successes to re-assure you that you can do it. Whether you think you can or you think you can't, the subconscious mind is designed to make sure that you are right. Your subconscious mind believes what your voice tells you more than anybody else's voice. What is it that you are saying to yourself? "Life and death are in your tongue" (Proverbs 18:21).

BONUS FROM JONAS
"You can language yourself to being lost, or you can language yourself into leaving a positive legacy!"

If you are going to achieve your worth, you must be willing to work harder on yourself than you work on your job. When you know your worth, then you will do the work. This work will determine your worth and your worth will determine your world. Let's use heating your house as an analogy. As the owner, you are in control of the temperature in your house; you preset it by setting the thermostat and thermometer gage. The thermostat produces the heat for the house and the thermometer controls how hot the house will become and reflects the level of heat that is in the house, preset by you. Wherever you have set the gage controls how hot the temperature in your house will get. Just as living your full potential is set by you, if you set your potential gage to a lower degree of achievement, then that is what you will produce. You are not getting what you deserve; you are getting exactly what you designed. However, when you get ready, just like with heating your house, you can also reset the gage by removing the restriction that you have placed on you to reach your highest positive potential. Move your potential gage higher.

BONUS FROM JONAS
"Things will become better as soon as you do!"

It's the same about your destiny. You determine how

high you want to go. If you rise higher than where you see yourself you will do negative and destructive things to sabotage yourself, to go back to a low level that you have pre-set. The same way that you control the temperature in your house is the same way that you control your destiny. You don't allow anyone else to manage that control. You must be willing to take responsibility for the level that you set your gage. You cannot overcome that setting unless you reset the gage.

It is not pre-set by anyone else but you. We came with unlimited potential within us. We came set with the gift. Set for greatness. We must cultivate what was given to us. Where have you set your gage? It takes personal maturity to see it for yourself and then go after it. Don't keep circling around the mountain. Time is up. Don't let your trip get cancelled.

Sometimes we label ourselves so that we can limit ourselves.

We cannot rise above our label. It is the way we see ourselves. It is our self-image. Our self-worth. We have allowed our life and conditioning to limit us. However, you are doing the work because you are worth it. If you don't get your worth together and you continue to believe that you are worthless, the outcome is always negative and destructive. Since we know that we are worth it, we are willing to do the work. And the work will have a positive impact on your world.

However, when you work on your worth, then your work will produce a different product. When you invest in your worth, it produces all the positive and productive outcomes for your life. You open up a new factory and that helps you to produce a new product. A new life. When you recognize your worth, you are tapping into your potential. This produces a new product; a new you and a new life. This book is designed to help you to be a victor and not a victim. To help you to rise. To empower you. To be your best self on purpose.

Our body is a covering to protect our real essence, our real jewel—our soul. You are not here by accident. You don't get a destructive life by default. You get a destructive life by design. It was designed by you.

But if you understand that you are worth it, then you become a self-fulfilling prophecy in a positive way. Now you build a more constructive life that you were designed and destined to achieve. It is not the things that we get in life that give us worth. It is the worth that we come with from our designer that makes the things that we have valuable. Worth is not external; it is internal. You came with the worth already built inside of you as a gift from your Creator. God has entrusted you with this worth to implement in your life and share it with others.

Perhaps you have heard about the concept of being a lifelong learner. Certainly, that is critical. However, what we want to introduce to you in this book is learning how to become a *laser learner*. Here is an example of how to become a laser learner: When you go to college, you must know what you are going in there for. If you don't, you are going to come out with something else. When you go into the supermarket, you must have a list to know what you will buy, or you will come out with everything but what you went in there for.

If you are a laser learner, you are learning specific skills that will help you live your purpose. A laser is very sharp, very focused, and very direct. On the other hand, when you are a lifelong learner, you are learning a lot of things, but you have to invest more time in deciphering the information and then determine what you will use and what you will throw out. It may even distract you, confuse you, and blur your vision. The cost is loss of time, loss of focus, loss of money, and loss of opportunity. It will cause you a delay in achieving your dreams. Becoming a laser learner, knowing your purpose will determine your focus. When you are a lifelong learner, you have the potential to become a wandering generality. But when you are a laser learner, you are a meaningful specific.

I encourage you to become a *laser learner*. To get where you need to go you can't fly all the time using panoramic lenses as a lifelong learner. I must zoom into my purpose, into my greatness, into my calling. When you don't understand the power of the laser learner, you go through life using your rearview mirror. You are looking at where you have been and not where you are going. As a laser learner, you are focusing on your future. You must be able to zoom in. And put on the zoom in lens like the eagle. When you are laser-focused you don't go into anything without knowing what you are going to get out of it.

"We are being bombarded with information, but are starving for knowledge." Just like the eagle stays focused on its prey, we must stay focused on our dreams. And because we are focused on our dreams, it causes us to cut through the fluff.

For example, have you ever gone to a fair or carnival and purchased a cotton candy? You purchase and begin to eat the cotton candy. Your sugar tolerance will determine how you will enjoy the cotton candy. For me, at first it tastes good. But in a short time it makes me sick. Because it is all fluff and no substance. This book is about substance that can and will transform your life. But you must be willing to move from where you are now to a new address. Some say what is that new address? I can't afford to move. You can't afford *not* to.

SLUMMY SIDE "I CAN'T DO AVENUE"	MOVE TO	SUNNY SIDE "I CAN DO BOULEVARD"
When I see a broken window, that is the slummy side.	⟶	Train some youth to become glass makers. That is the sunny side.
When I see a missing brick, that is the slummy side.	⟶	Let some youth into the union and help them to become masons and builders. That is the sunny side.
When I see a missing door, that is the slummy side.	⟶	Train some youth to become carpenters. That is the sunny side.
When I see vulgar words, profanity, and graffiti, that is the slummy side.	⟶	Train some youth to become painters or artists. That is the sunny side.

BONUS FROM JONAS
"You have to move from I can't do avenue, over to I can do boulevard."

There is a *brighter* day ahead.

BONUS FROM JONAS
Move over to "I can do boulevard." There you will discover that "your future is so bright that you are going to need sunglasses!"

In order to do that...

BONUS FROM JONAS
"You must have a check up from the neck up."

The following questions still remain. Why are you reading this book? Why are you listening to motivational CDs? Why are you watching DVDs?

Why do you want to open up that business? If you know the why, you'll do whatever it takes that is positive to get to the how. The how may get you a job. But the why will cause you to own your own company. However, the question is: Is it worth it? And if the answer is yes, then you'll do the work. As the scripture says in Proverbs 23:7, "As a man thinketh in his heart, so is he/she."

Romans 12:2 states: "Be not conformed to this world, but be ye transformed by the renewing of your mind." In order to be transformed, you must first be properly informed. This is what this book will do for you...If you let it. You must be willing "to take a chance, take charge and take control of your life." Because...

BONUS FROM JONAS
"If it's going to be, it's up to me. If you are going to get through, it's up to you. You are the magic."

There are five kinds of people: wishers, weepers, worriers, warriors, and winners. Which one are you?

Wishers. These people sit around wishing for a better life, job, and relationship, wishing for more money, or a better home, or a better education. But it's not going to happen by wishing.

BONUS FROM JONAS
"A lot of people go through life depending on their wishbone instead of depending on their backbone."

Stop vacillating with wishes and start standing firm and utilizing your backbone. Do the work because you are worth it.

Weepers. Weepers are crying about everything. Some are crying because we are in a recession, some are crying about being in a depression. They are crying about the economy, they are crying about their jobs, they are crying about the world in general.

But it is time to dry your tears. Get up off of the stool of do-nothing and accept responsibility for your life. Make a decision that you are no longer going to be a spectator on the bleachers of life, but you are coming out. I am calling you out on the field of life, and challenging you to become a participant. The scripture says, "Weeping may endure for a night, but joy cometh in the morning" (Psalms 30:5). It's morning time.

Worriers. There are two things that you should never worry about. (1) That which you cannot help. My father died when I was a little boy. In growing up, I always wondered what it would have been like if I had a father. But there was nothing I could do about it. (2) The second thing that you should never worry about is that which you can help. If you can help the situation, then get up and help it.

BONUS FROM JONAS
"Worrying is like a rocking chair. It gives you something to do but you are not getting anywhere!"

BONUS FROM JONAS
"You are next in line for a blessing! Don't get out of line, don't detour and don't allow anyone to cut in front of you...it's full steam ahead." Because "whatever you focus on the longest becomes the strongest!"

Warriors. When I talk about warriors, I am not talking about fighting with bullets, bombs, and being a bully. I am talking about taking your life back, holding yourself accountable for who you are and whose you are.

When you take your life back you must re-design a positive life to gain your victory. "The easiest way for evil to take over is for righteous people to do nothing." You are not going to win if you are not willing to fight. And it is fighting time. And while you fight, you must stay focused. You must know what you are fighting for. If you don't know what you are fighting for, you won't fight for long. Everything that is worth having and keeping of great value is worth fighting for. When you are dressed for spiritual success and you do it God's way, the scripture says, "No weapon formed against me shall prosper" (Isaiah 54:17). Stand firm with confidence and have the positive attitude that when the enemy is coming from the south, the north, the east and the west, "I am not going to let any of you escape." You've got to fight for your better life.

Fight for righteousness with integrity and maintain your character.

BONUS FROM JONAS
"Courage is not the absence of fear; courage is doing what you need to do—when you need to do it— in spite of fear."

BONUS FROM JONAS
"You cannot defeat what you do not confront!"

BONUS FROM JONAS
"Yesterday is a cancelled check. Tomorrow is a promissory note. But today you have cash in your hand; spend it wisely because today is the first day of the rest of your life!"

If someone gives you $486,000 with one stipulation— you must spend it all within 24 hours of receiving it—what would you do with it? How would you spend it? Would you buy a Rolls Royce, a Mercedes Benz, or a Cadillac? Would you build a beautiful home in the country, take a luxurious vacation cruise, go on a huge shopping spree or invest in the stock market? You will do whatever you can because you don't want to lose any of the money. You will spend it all in one day because if you don't use it, you'll lose it.

On the other hand, you are given as a gift 486,000 seconds everyday. What are you doing with those precious life giving moments? How are you investing them? Are you spending them without thought or plan, or are you using them purposefully? Now we are given 486,000 seconds every 24 hours. And when you don't use them, you lose them. They are gone forever. Are you living your purpose; your dreams, goals, and aspirations? If you don't use them, you'll lose them. So there is urgency to use up every bit of your 486,000 seconds that God gave to you as a gift every day. These seconds are precious and priceless. And every moment counts. They are not transferable. You can't save them. "...For what is your life? It is even as a vapor, that appears for a little while and then 'poof' vanishes away" (James 4:14). Now that you neglected to use them wisely, you are choking on regrets and now you are talking about what should have been, would have been, or could have been. Then you start singing the lyrics of an old song: "If I could turn back the hands of time." But you can't.

BONUS FROM JONAS
"Live everyday like it is your last day because one of these days you will be right."

Winners. These are the individuals who do not let things happen. They make positive things happen. They understand that they are the CEOs of their lives. They realize that...

BONUS FROM JONAS
"Some will, some won't. So what! Stop whining, stop weeping, and start winning! Next!"

BONUS FROM JONAS
"A setback is really a step back to prepare yourself to make a greater comeback!"

When life throws bricks at you, you have learned the art of how to catch those bricks and build a solid foundation. "Now you are standing on the promises and not just sitting on the premises." When life throws lemons at you, learn the art of how to catch those lemons and make lemonade, and have yourself a spiritual party. However, don't drink all of the lemonade at your party. Open up a lemonade stand and make yourself some profit. After that, life stops throwing lemons at you because you are being too productive. To make lemonade, you have to go and buy your own lemons. Life was throwing lemons at you to limit you. Now that you have learned how to utilize the lemons in a positive way, if you want more lemons for your lemonade, you have to go out and buy them.

"People are always blaming their circumstances for what they are. I don't believe in circumstances. The people who get on in this world are the people who get up and look for the circumstances they want, and, if they can't find them, make them."— George Bernard Shaw

Vision, Value, and Voice
Vision

As we stated earlier, the eagles have extraordinary vision. The scripture says "Where there is no vision, the people perish" (Proverbs 29:18). I believe most people don't have a large enough vision of themselves, and they suffer from low self-esteem. Self-esteem is one of the most important ingredients needed in our lives today.

My definition of self-esteem is how you see, feel and think about yourself.

I am sharing with you the three Vs of building high and healthy self-esteem. It is how you see yourself, your *vision.* How you feel about yourself, your *value,* and how you think about yourself, your *voice.* It is not about focusing on the external. It focuses on the internal. *You.* How is your vision? Is it 20/20?

Vision in this context does not deal with eyesight only, but it has to do with insight and foresight as well.

A young reporter looking to make a name for himself ran up to Ms. Helen Keller. He said to Ms. Keller, "Life must have been very difficult for you. Being blind and not able to see." Helen Keller said to him, "Worse than being blind is having sight but no vision." He had come from the perspective that being blind was merely a physical thing. Are you able to see your future? Or is someone or something blocking your view? One of the things that I have learned is what Peter Drucker said:
"The best way to predict the future is to create it."

That is why as I indicated earlier, it is important to get a larger vision of yourself. Again, it is important to ask these questions: Where are you now? Where are you going? How are you planning on getting there? "With no vision, the dream will perish. With a positive vision and action, your dreams will flourish." You cannot rise higher than your vision for yourself.

In order to achieve your vision it is critical that you surround yourself with people who believe in you and who are willing to invest in you in a positive way to help you bring your vision to reality. "One is too small of a number to achieve greatness."

Feelings contribute to your self-esteem just as logic and facts do. However, most people with low self-esteem seek to drive their vehicles in life, using feelings only. Feelings are important and need to be in the vehicle, but...

BONUS FROM JONAS
"Feelings make a wonderful passenger, but a lousy driver. Feelings are a reckless driver, seeking desperately a place to have an accident."

Grandma Moses always had the desire at an early age to paint. But she was told that what she needed to do was to get married and have a family. And she did that. However, throughout their marriage they struggled financially and there came a time when her husband died and all of her children were grown and gone. It was then that Grandma Moses returned to the dream that she had in her. The dream that she had suppressed. It had been lying dormant in her, gasping to be free.

She used what she had in her hand. It was a paintbrush. Then she started to paint. And the first painting she painted at 75 years old earned her more money than she and her husband earned together for their entire life.

I am not knocking marriage and family. It is wonderful. It wasn't either/or. It was supposed to have been both. Just think of what she and her husband could have achieved together had she followed her dream while developing her marriage and growing her family. Think of how many others would have been blessed had she cultivated her purpose in her marriage.

BONUS FROM JONAS
"It takes money to run a poor house!"

It has been said, "Money isn't everything. But it is right up there with oxygen! You need it!" The scriptures say, "…Money answers all things!" (Ecclesiastes 10:19).

It doesn't matter what is in your hands, but what does matter is what you are going to do with it. Are you using all of what is in your hands to make your dreams come true? To create a positive future for *you*. After all, that is where we are going to spend the rest of our lives.

"If you spend five minutes complaining you have wasted five minutes and you may have started what is known as a financial cancer of the bones. They will haul you off to a financial desert and there let you choke on the dust of your own regrets."—Jim Rohn

Many people are perishing because they have given up. They have created an environment where they learned helplessness and hopelessness. This book offers *hope*. The word hope spelled in acrostics means:

Having
Only
Positive
Expectations for you.

Sometimes when I travel across the country, I see people who have given up. So many people today in this great, grand, and glorious country that we are privileged to live in have

20/20 eyesight but no vision.

That is why so many are perishing. But Proverbs 29:18 also suggests that with vision, my people will flourish.

BONUS FROM JONAS
"If you don't like who you are, or where you are, you are not stuck with who you are or where you are. You have the power to take your life back again!"

When you take your life back then you can help create a world where everybody is somebody. For, if I hold up one of my hands there are five fingers on it. As long as those five fingers are divided you cannot successfully make a positive impact on the world. But if you put all five of those fingers together, then you have a powerful fist. Then, you can knock out hopelessness and helplessness. You can help eliminate inferiority complexes. You can help stomp out violence, drugs, and alcoholism.

It was once said that, "Coming together is the beginning, staying together is progress, and working together is success."—Henry Ford. But here are some things that we must do.

It starts with me. Then it moves to we. We must develop teachers who would teach. Not just to make a living, but to teach because it is their life. If we could only produce doctors who are more concerned about public health and not personal wealth. We need lawyers who are more concerned about justice than a judgeship. We need more preachers who preach for the promises, not for the profit only. And, if only mothers and fathers would understand that the best lessons are better caught, than taught. It is important that parents love one another and their children unconditionally.

It is essential that we also deal with the "me." That we learn how to love ourselves first before we can love anyone else. And we are not talking about selfishness; we are talking about the love that is essential.

LOVE spelled out in acrostics means:

Listen
Overlook
Voice of Approval
Extra Mile

Listen

Be willing to listen to one another. We were given two ears and one mouth, which says to me that we should listen twice as much as we talk. One study in America indicates that we have to repeat a particular thing seven times before it is heard because we simply do not listen. And, of course, there is a difference between hearing and listening. Allow me to make this distinction. If everything is working properly with your ears, you can hear sound, but listening is a choice. You must choose to listen.

Overlook

We have to be willing to overlook some things. What I have observed in life is that far too many times we talk about all of the things that are wrong with an individual and we do not spend any time talking about what is right with the person. What we need to do is praise those people in our lives.

Voice of Approval

We must be willing to give our voice of approval. Every person should have at least one person in their life who knows all about them and still loves them anyway —unconditionally. So give your voice. Give yourself permission to succeed. Say **yes** to your success. Sometimes we look for approval outside of ourselves only. Or we look for someone else to give us permission to succeed. But we refuse to give ourselves our own voice of approval. As I said earlier, your subconscious mind believes your voice more quickly than it believes someone else's. Your subconscious cannot distinguish between truth and error.

A study indicates that 87 percent of people talk to themselves: Your own voice has a greater impact on you than anyone else's voice. If it is a positive message, then the results are positive, and if it's a negative message, then the results are negative. What is it that you are saying to yourself? What you say to yourself determines your results. What I have discovered, if we are not careful, we talk ourselves out of our dreams. Sometimes we see it for others, but it is time now for us to see it for ourselves. So don't tell yourself what you can't do but tell yourself what you can do, with the proper knowledge and skills and then, *do it*. And since you talk to yourself every day anyway, what is it that you are saying to yourself? Give yourself your own voice of approval.

Believe in yourself with confidence.

BONUS FROM JONAS
"Most people are educated way beyond their level of execution. Do what you know, learn as you go, and you will grow!"

Extra Mile

We must also be willing to go the extra mile for one another. One of the things that I'm learning in life is that, in traveling that road, there is less traffic because most people, unfortunately, are not willing to go the extra mile.

Value

BONUS FROM JONAS
"When your *value* is clear, your decision is easy!"

When you value yourself, you are building high and healthy self-esteem, what is important to you. What you value defines *you*. Your value is your anchor, your foundational block. It is your guiding light, your compass.

It is what helps you to navigate through the storms of life. You will not get lost if you have identified your true *value*. I challenge you to define your value, because if you don't you will be following someone else's. You are special and biologically unique. Define your value:

_____

_____

_____

_____

_____

You owe it to yourself and to the world to honor your values and demonstrate your uniqueness. To be your best self on purpose. When you identify and honor your worth to yourself, it is easy to identify and articulate your worth to the world.

Why We Should Value Faith, Family, and Friends

Our faith must be rooted in absolutes. "Faith is the substance of things hoped for and the evidence of things not seen" (Hebrews 11:1). The scripture states that faith is the "substance." That is a compound word. The first part of the word is "sub" which means to go under. Faith is like a submarine that goes under the water, a subway that goes under the ground. The second part of the word is "stance," which causes us to stand. It goes to the very core of our belief system. Our faith extends to our core beliefs. It is what causes us to stand regardless of what is going on around us. It has nothing to do with what is going on outside of us, but rather, what is going on inside of us. It is learning to do without while our faith is "doing" within. This is the foundation of our very being. Luke said, "It is in Him that we live and move and have our very being." (Acts 17:28). That is why our faith must be grounded in absolutes. It is the thing that we believe, that causes us to *stand*. It motivates us to move forward with positive action: "Because we walk by faith and not by sight" (2 Corin.5:7). In other words, our faith must have feet.

BONUS FROM JONAS
"Sometimes faith can be the enemy of human facts!"

James 2:17-18 states, "Show me your faith without your work and I will show you my faith by my work." In essence he is saying: "Show me what you got!" And when we demonstrate our faith, we will realize that "all things are possible, for those who believe." Faith doesn't become real until you demonstrate it. The intellectual faith in our heads must travel 18 inches from our heads to our hearts that will create a heart of love and compassion. From the heart it travels a little further to engage our hands.

Then we go to work demonstrating our faith in a positive way. We will use our hands to help ourselves and then reach out to help others. Then we are prepared to:

BONUS FROM JONAS
"Each one, reach one, teach one, and keep one!"

The eagle also has faith: He just doesn't think it. He believes it and then he demonstrates it.

An eagle values other eagles and they are committed to their families. Some eagles build their nests in high mountains or in tall, sturdy and strong trees. They gather all of the materials for the nest themselves in preparation for their eaglets. Most eagles do not eat dead animals. For example, one type of eagle will only eat fresh salmon fish. And, of course, they deliver it to the eaglets. In order to feed them, they take the food from their mouth and put it in the mouths of their babies. This demonstrates the caring nature of the eagle for its family. However, when it is time to teach the eaglets/babies how to fly, they do not decide to fly on their own. They are actually pushed out of the nest!

Even eagles need a push.

BONUS FROM JONAS
"The only way an eagle learns how to fly is by falling!"

Mommy and Daddy eagle start to dismantle the nest, which indicates that they will not need it anymore. The mother and father eagle work together to teach the eaglets how to fly. They take the eaglets one by one from the highest point, a mountain or tall tree. Sometimes the mother eagle takes them on her back high in the sky and she drops them. And, of course, when she drops them the eaglets are going down—fast! And the mother eagle looks at the father eagle and says, "What do you think? Do you think Junior is going to make it?" The father eagle says, "It doesn't look good. I better go and get him."

However, the father waits until the very last minute because eagles have the ability to fly about 200 miles per hour. So Daddy eagle swoops down and catches Junior just in time! And, of course, Junior gives a sigh of relief.

He says, "Oh, thank you, Daddy. I was a little worried. I am so glad you got me. I am so glad this is over." But it is not over. The daddy eagle takes him back to the mountaintop and drops him again. The same thing happens again and the father catches him a second time. Now Junior is saying, "This isn't funny; I don't like this game anymore." The parents continue the process until Junior sticks out his wings and flies.

This is how we as humans are to love and cherish our families as well. And, when it comes to us, in most cases, we just need to be pushed out of our comfort zone. Many times we are not aware that we can fly. We are designed to fly, not fall. We are designed to climb, not crawl. We are designed to soar, not sink. Just like the mother and father eagles taught the eaglet how to fly, this book is designed to teach you and your family how to fly, as well. However, you have to decide that you are going to be the eagle that you were designed to be.

BONUS FROM JONAS
"If you want to do something that you have never done before, you must become the person that you have never been before."

Insanity can be defined as doing the same thing over and over again, yet expecting different results. If you want a different result, then do things differently.

BONUS FROM JONAS
"Lessons are repeated until learned."

How long would you want to be in the twelfth grade? One year is enough. Often, the reason we repeat lessons over and over again is because we did not get the lesson the first time. There are at least two essential principles that I want you to get from this book: roots and wings.

Roots are your value system. What is your anchor? Why are you here? Where have you been? Where are you going? What is your purpose and your plan to get there? These are essential questions that you must ask and answer for yourself.

BONUS FROM JONAS
"Fruits are seasonal but roots are permanent. If you are not getting the kind of fruit that you desire and deserve, then cultivate your roots."

Wings give you the ability to fly. I am going to teach you how to fly again.

So that you might release that eagle spirit that has been lying dormant in you. In order to release that eagle spirit, sometimes we need help from a friend.

True friends are like angels...

"I believe that friends are quiet angels who lift us to our feet when our wings have trouble remembering how to fly."— Unknown

BONUS FROM JONAS
**"I am your friend and I want you to know that...
You are a manuscript that has not yet been published.
You are a poem that has not yet been composed.
You are a song that has not yet been sung.
You are a dream that has not yet been fulfilled.
You are a vision that has not yet happened.
Your future which has not yet come to pass.
You are a miracle waiting to explode."**

This is your time "to bud, to bloom and to blossom" into a bright and beautiful future. You have been placed on the center stage of life. The curtain has been pulled...

It's show time. It is time to shine and to share your story.

Many people have written a script for you and convinced you that you are perhaps a chicken, turkey, or even a vulture. But I suggest to you to tear up the script they have written for you, for your past does not have to equal your future. That was then, and this is *now*. Use your past as a school. Learn from it. Learn that failure is an event, not a person.

When you fail this gives you an opportunity to start all over again, more intelligently. You have been given a new, clean canvas, a new beginning and I don't know about your past, I don't even know about your present, but what I do know is that your future is spotless. This book will teach you how to grow, glow and how to go.

You have heard the saying, "One for the money, two for the show, three to get ready and..." Most of the time we get stuck in this phase (three to get ready).

I am going to write that book one of these days
   ...Three to get ready...
I am going to go back to school one of these days
   ...Three to get ready...
I am going to get married one of these days
   ...Three to get ready...
I am going to open up my own business one of these days
   (...Three to get ready...well)

"One for the money, two for the show, three to get ready," and...I am stopping by to let you know—Four. It's time for you to get up and go!

Get up and get going and create the kind of life that you desire and that you deserve.

It is important also that you implement the three Ps: *purpose, passion,* and *plan* into your life.

Purpose

What is your purpose? Your purpose is your reason for living.

"This is the true joy in life: Being used for a purpose recognized by yourself as a mighty one, being a force of nature instead of a feverish, selfish clod of ailments and grievances, complaining that the world will not devote itself to making you happy. I am of the opinion that my life belongs to the whole community, and as long as I live, it is my privilege to do for it what I can. It is a sort of splendid torch, which I have got hold of for the moment and I want to make it burn as brightly as possible before handing it on to future generations."—George Bernard Shaw

Each of us has been given a torch. We are responsible to keep our torch lit and to light as many other people's torches as possible. That is why I am so fired up. I want to help light as many other people's torches as I can. If my candle is lit and you approach me and your candle is out and you ask for a light and I give you a light, that doesn't reduce my light. In fact, I have learned that if I take my candle and light your candle that together we create a brighter and better world.

Mother Theresa once said, "I can't do what you can do, you can't do what I can do. But together, we can do great things."

Far too many people die with their purpose still in them. In fact, I believe that the richest place in this country, unfortunately, is in the graveyard. It is there that you will find so many books that were never written, so many songs never sung, so many businesses that never came into fruition, so many dreams died and are buried in the graveyard. Don't let your dreams, your goals and your aspirations die in you.

Live your purpose with a passion.

Because, you owe it to *God.* You owe it to *yourself.*

You owe it to your *family.*

You owe it to your *community.*

You owe it to the world to be the best that you can be. Your life is a gift from God and what you make of life is your gift back to Him. What kind of gift are you giving? If you choose not to utilize your time, talents, and treasures, everyone suffers. "A man's gifts maketh room for him and bringeth him before great men" (Proverbs 18:16).

BONUS FROM JONAS
"Don't let anyone bury you until after you are dead. You are bigger than that, you are better than that and the best is still in you."

Some might ask, "So what do you mean by that?" It is my goal to leave all of the good that I have done to the next generation. I want someone to be able to say that "I have fought the good fight, I've finished my course and I have kept the faith." For, I have lived a positive and productive life. No regrets. My goal is to make a positive difference and not just a dent.

We were given a life and it is time for each of us to live it.

I love what Dr. Benjamin Mays says in "Just A Minute."
"I have only just a minute,
Only sixty seconds in it;
Forced upon me, can't refuse it.
Didn't seek it, didn't choose it.
But it is up to me to use it.
I must suffer if I lose it.
Give account if I abuse it.
Just a tiny little minute.
But eternity is in it."

We are running out of time. I don't know how many seconds, minutes, hours, days, weeks, months, or years we have left. But I do know one thing: We are running out of time and it is later now than ever before. What time is it? It's Now O'Clock!

Do It Now! Nothing in the world can take the place of
Persistence.
Talent Will Not
Nothing is more common than unsuccessful men
with talent.
Genius Will Not
Unrewarded Genius Is Almost A Proverb.
Education Will Not
The World is full of educated derelicts.
Persistence and Determination Alone Are Omnipotent.
—Former President Calvin Coolidge

Why *now*? Because...

BONUS FROM JONAS
"We have a date with our divine destiny!"

Passion

Once you have discovered what your purpose is, then you must live it with a passion. Passion can be defined as a driving force. It is a burning fire in your belly. You love it. When you know what your passion is and are living it, I can call you at any time and you are ready to go. You don't need anyone to turn you on. For example...

BONUS FROM JONAS
"As a motivational speaker, I love speaking so much that I am willing to do it for free. But because I am so good at it, they are willing to pay me."

BONUS FROM JONAS
"Your career is what you are paid for...
Your purpose is what you are made for."

Plan

You have probably heard it said that "You plan your work then you work your plan." Most of my life I was following someone else's plan. Finally, I realized that I had the wrong plan. It was their plan, not mine. If you do not have your own plan, you are doomed to spend the rest of your life living someone else's.

Several years ago, I drove home to South Carolina to celebrate my mother's eightieth birthday. One of the things I did before leaving Rochester was to purchase a map and develop a plan. I mapped out my trip to South Carolina and back. Most people will plan vacation and follow their maps. Yet, tragically, many have never taken the time to design their own lives. Don't you think it is time to create a map for your life? Don't you think it is time to develop your own plan?

"It must be born in mind that the tragedy of life does not lie in not reaching your goals. The tragedy lies in not having any goals to reach. It is not calamity to die with dreams unfulfilled, but it is a calamity not to dream. It is not a disaster to be unable to capture your ideals, but it is a disaster to have no ideal to capture. It is not a disgrace not to reach the stars, but it is a disgrace to have no stars to reach." —Dr. Benjamin Mays.

BONUS FROM JONAS
"The greatest enemy to our dreams is not that we aim too high and miss; it is that we aim too low and hit."

In order to live your purpose with a passion you must set SMART goals. A study was done at Yale University on the graduating class of 1952. Only 3 percent of the class had written down their goals. They followed that class until 1972. 20 years later. What they discovered was that the 3 percent of the class who had written down their goals had achieved more financially than the other 97 percent combined. I am a strong advocate for goal setting.

"Write the vision, make it plain and run with it" (Habakkuk 2:2).

BONUS FROM JONAS
"If you think it, ink it. Write it down then get it done!"

In acrostics, SMART goals are
Specific
Measurable
Attainable
Relevant, and with a
Timetable.

Specific

Your goals must be specific. Specific means that you are clear on what your goal is and what it is going to take to bring it into reality. In order to illustrate this; let us look at the following example. You decide that you must lose 30 pounds. Again, the 30 pounds is specific. In order to achieve that weight reduction there are some things you must do.

First, exercise at least 20 to 30 minutes per day, at least three times a week, with a built in five-minute warm up and cool down. Second, avoid fast food. Next, increase your vegetable, fruit and water intake. The whole objective is to eat in moderation. This is an example, and it is applicable to any goal that you set for yourself.

I know it is hard to do, for we live in a wonderful country where two industries thrive with two different goals and results: Fast food restaurants and fast weight loss clinics. I am keenly aware that we are living in what I call a microwave society. The quick fix. Some people would rather pop a pill to lose weight overnight and wake up the next morning with all of their unwanted pounds gone. Yet, you know and I know that this is not a safe way to lose weight.

BONUS FROM JONAS
"Inch by inch is a cinch. Yard by yard is hard.
Keep on inching." Someone might say,
"How do you eat an elephant?"

Of course I'm not into elephant eating, but one bite at a time.

Measurable

A goal must be measurable. I have learned with my corporate background that whatever is measured gets done. Let's go back to our weight loss example about losing 30 pounds. What is your present weight? Say, for example you weigh 200 pounds. That means 170 pounds is your ultimate goal.

Attainable

Setting a goal is necessary. However, that goal must be realistic. In other words, it must be attainable. Are you able to reach it? A more important question is, can you lose 30 pounds in a week? The answer is no. Can you do it in one year in a healthy and safe manner? Yes, you can!

Relevant

Sometimes the things that we do should never have been done in the first place, for it was not relevant to our goals. Someone wisely said, "Things that matter the most should never be left to the mercy of things that matter the least." In this case, good health matters most, for everything else that you want to achieve is predicated upon good health. Based on the following reports from medical professionals,

"Men in poor physical condition are four times more likely to die from a heart attack than those who are physically fit."—Dr. Lars Ekelund, Duke University Medical Center

BONUS FROM JONAS
"In my opinion, there isn't any great reward being the richest person in the cemetery."

"People who cannot find time for recreation are obligated sooner or later to find time for illness." —John Wanamaker, Philadelphia department store

"Exercise during middle age can actually retard physiological aging. Activity seems to lengthen life, maybe one or two years. We can expect that for every hour you're active, you will get to live that hour over. And possibly two more on top of that." — Dr. Ralph S. Paffenbarger, Jr., Stanford School of Medicine

It has been said that every year 91 million people make New Year's resolutions and 70 million people break them in the first week. They gave up because they did not follow through. 70 million people gave up on their goals. They quit!

BONUS FROM JONAS
"The fortune is in the follow through!"

According to a survey done by the *Daily Times* (1996) 33 percent of American workers plan their daily schedules. Another 45 percent of American workers make a plan once a week, but only 9 percent complete their plan. Whether you are working to get rid of unwanted pounds, or living your purpose in life, here is a plan that can help you achieve your goals.

There are seven steps to setting goals:

1. Identify your goal.
2. Set a deadline.
3. List the obstacles that you must overcome in order to achieve your goals.
4. Identify the people/groups that you will need to get help from.
5. List the skills that you will need to get in order to realize your goals.
6. Develop an action plan.
7. List the benefits...what is in it for you.

In addition, there are short and long-term goals. And, of course, when you are asking yourself the above questions, you should consider which kind of goal you are setting: Short or Long term.

Short Term Goals are three months to one year. **Long Term Goals** can be anywhere from 2-10 years. There are also give-up goals. On the give-up goals, tell everybody, because people are more supportive in what you want to give up. However, Go-up goals should only be shared with the individuals who love and believe in you, and are willing to help you achieve those goals.

BONUS FROM JONAS
"Always reach for the moon. And, if you miss the moon, you will fall among the stars. And after all, that is great company."

There are five questions you must ask yourself about goals, and the answer must be yes to all five.
1. Is it really my goal?
2. Are my short and long term goals consistent with one another?
3. Is it morally right and fair?
4. Can I commit myself emotionally to complete the plan?
5. Can I visualize myself reaching my goal?

There are seven types of goals that each person needs to be concerned about:

The Seven Types of Goals Are	1—Spiritual Goals	2—Family Goals	3—Physical Goals
4—Intellectual Goals	5—Relational Goals	6—Career Goals	7—Financial Goals

As you read this part of the book about goal setting, you noticed that I purposefully spent a lot of time on SMART goals. As I have indicated before, most people spend a lot of time planning their vacations but have not designed a plan for their lives. You have heard it said that, "If you don't know where you are going, any road will take you there." However, if you follow these time-tested techniques that are in my book, they can help you achieve your dreams, goals, and aspirations...if you do them."

Dr. Martin Luther King, Jr., said, "The time is always ripe to do what is right."

It is right to have and live your dreams.

Time Table

You must have a specific time when your goal starts and when it ends.

There are some critical things to remember when setting goals. These three Ps will help: personal, positive, and present tense. We must make our goals *personal*.

We must take ownership. They have to be ours. Secondly, we must be *positive*. Believe that we can do it and get the skills necessary to make it happen.

BONUS FROM JONAS
"If the only tool you have in your tool box is a hammer, you'll have the tendency to think that everything is a nail."

Your goals must be spoken in the *present tense*. For example...I am 170 pounds. I am a doctor. I am a motivational speaker. I am an author...not going to be, I am right now. You must be able to see the invisible, to hear the inaudible, to touch the intangible, and then you will be able to do the impossible.

BONUS FROM JONAS
"Act the way you want to be and soon you will be the way that you act."

Three Action Steps

In order to implement a new positive behavior/habit that leads to the new you, you must practice the 90-day principle that will help you to create the new life that you desire and that you deserve.

Take these Three Action Steps:

(1) Eliminate: The first 30 days deals with eliminating bad, negative, toxic thinking, behavior, and people. Are these things and people taking you up or pulling you down?
Do an evaluation. Are the people in your life taking you closer to your goal or moving you further away from it? Where are they taking you?

(2) Implement: The second 30 days you are learning new positive habits, behavior, skills, and disciplines. You are creating and turning that new habit into a new discipline. Implement the new habit—Discipline.

(3) Demonstrate: The last 30 days deals with demonstrating the new positive knowledge, skills, and discipline that create new habits, new behavior, and new discipline that you have learned—walking in the newness of life. It will propel you to create a positive new life—a new beginning. You have a new positive behavior in your new positive lifestyle, which will lead you to positive action.

BONUS FROM JONAS
"You must face it in order to erase it!"

Chapter Three

Attitude, Aptitude, Altitude

A. Attitude

The "A" is for Attitude. This chapter deals with Attitude, Aptitude and Altitude. The eagle has an attitude of "I can do it." A positive, "Yes, I can" attitude versus a "No, I can't" attitude. You can develop an attitude that will make you successful.

Just like the eagle. Yes, you can do it too!

The Human Aspect

There are three essential "As" each human being must incorporate in their personal and professional lives in order to reach their highest potential. That will help them to "dare to dream and then to do it." In this chapter you will learn the importance of having a proper attitude. It is your Attitude, not your Aptitude that will determine your Altitude. You will learn that you were born with an eagle spirit within. And that each one of us needs to be taught how to fly again. Sometimes we let environment, upbringing, previous beliefs, education, the economy, bad relationships, domineering bosses on the job, and poison people steal our dreams.

As I said earlier, I am originally from South Carolina. There we had a bug spray called Black Flag. The purpose of this spray was to kill the flies, mosquitoes, gnats, and other bugs. Long after I stopped spraying the negative odor lingered.

45

The point that I am making is this: Negative people can kill you. And they can kill you graveyard dead. They can kill your dreams. They can cause you to settle for a life of mediocrity. They can cause you to die with your dreams still in you... Don't let them. You deserve to live your dreams. When you stay around what I call poison people, long after they are gone the affects of their negativity continues to affect your life in a negative way if you let it.

BONUS FROM JONAS
"Some people are so negative they walk into a dark room and they begin to develop."

It is time to get a New Attitude. "Dare to dream and then do it!" What is your dream? What is it that you want to be? What is it that you want to do? What is it that you want to have? Most people have heard Dr. Martin Luther King's famous speech, "I Have a Dream!" A part of that powerful, life-changing speech was "to create a world for his four, little children that they would be able to live in a world and not be judged by the color of their skin, but by the content of their character." Powerful! Unfortunately, far too many people are giving and living a speech called, "I *had* a dream." They have stopped dreaming. They have given up. But one of the reasons that I wrote this book is to help as many people as I can to dream again. And I am starting with *you!*

There are five types of dreamers that I identify in this chapter: dream fakers, dream breakers, dream bakers, dream undertakers, and dream makers.

Dream fakers are the great pretenders. They talk right, but walk left. I am sure you have heard the saying, "Fake it until you make it." As I always say, "You can make it, and *never* have to fake it." They spend so much time faking it that they never make it. I am encouraging you to be a maker of your dreams and not a faker.

BONUS FROM JONAS
"If you don't live your dreams you are doomed to spend the rest of your life living someone else's."

Dream breakers don't finish anything that they start. They look for anyone else who has a dream so that they can discourage them...They will break your dreams, goals and aspirations. "They came to steal, to kill, and to destroy."

They can't see it for themselves and they definitely don't want to see it for you. There's an old saying that "misery loves company." If you want your dreams to become a reality, don't keep company with dream breakers. As you read this book remember that

BONUS FROM JONAS
"A chapter a day keeps mediocrity away and welcomes in greatness to stay. Welcome in greatness!"

Dream bakers are always cooking up something. They always have something in the oven, but it never seems to get done cooking. They are never willing to get all of the proper ingredients. They confuse activity with accomplishment. That reminds me of a true story that illustrates this point.

I bought my first home in Rochester, New York, where it seems as if it snows nine months out of the year. One particular morning, it was extremely cold and snowing heavily. The wind was blowing and it was time for me to go to work.

Of course my car was in my driveway covered with a lot of snow and ice. On each side of the driveway were houses, each with hedges, which blocked my view. So I cleaned off my car and decided that I was not going to shovel the driveway. My plan was to get in the car, start and let it warm up and step on the accelerator to get out of the driveway in a hurry. But before I did that, I started thinking that maybe there might be a car coming down the street and that I would back into the street and the car would hit me. I thought I should take a look first. I did and it was clear in both directions.

I got in the car with haste, put it in reverse, and pressed down on the accelerator.

I was making good progress, or so I thought. Suddenly a thought came to mind that maybe there is a car coming now. So I stopped in the slope of the driveway. I got out of the car to see if a car was coming and there was not one coming. I got back into the car and put it in reverse again and pressed on the accelerator only to discover that I was stuck.

I was determined not to do any shoveling that morning. I came up with a brilliant plan. Or so I thought. I kept on pressing the accelerator. I watched the speedometer. It first started out at 10 miles per hour, then 20, then 30, and then 40.

No doubt that it probably went as high as 70 miles per hour. But I was still stuck.

The tires were spinning fast. There was a lot of activity, but I was not going anywhere. There was a lot of activity, but no accomplishment.

That is what happens when you are a dream baker. You confuse activity with accomplishment.

BONUS FROM JONAS
"You are all dressed up with no place to go."

Dream undertakers are the individuals who do not want anything out of life. And, they do not want you to have anything either. You may have high positive thoughts, but their goal is to bring you down. Why? They think down, they feel down, they act down, they live down and they want to bring *you* down. That is why they are called the undertakers. Undertakers allowed life and living to stop them from being alive. The African-American novelist Richard Wright said that, "The impulse to dream had been slowly beaten out of me by experience..." Don't let undertakers take you under.

Dream makers make things happen. They are the ones who illustrate my saying: "Teamwork makes the dream work." And as I always say,

BONUS FROM JONAS
"There are three kinds of people. Those who make things happen, those who watch things happen and those who wondered what happened."

I am a dream maker. I make positive things happen. That is one of the reasons why you are reading this book. I believe that *you* are a dream maker, too.

I encourage you not to go where the path may lead you, but be willing to go where there is no path and leave a trail. Be a trailblazer. Remember, we can't do it alone. We all need some help. I love what Alex Haley said:

"Any time you see a turtle on a fence post, you know he had some help." There are a lot of people who have helped me. So I want to help you, too. Actually, I am standing on the shoulders of all of my ancestors. All that I am, or ever hope to be, I owe to God, my mother, and others.

A dream maker does not allow his dreams to be deferred. Langston Hughes wrote a powerful, potent poem concerning your dreams.

What Happens to a Dream Deferred
"Does it dry up
Like a raisin in the sun?
Or fester like a sore.
And then run?
Does it stink like rotten meat?
Or crust and sugar over.
Like a syrupy sweet?
Maybe it just sags
Like a heavy load
Or does it explode?"

Don't let your dream die in you.

I just covered the five kinds of dreamers. One of the key lessons that I want you to know is that your attitude reveals where you have been, where you are, and will determine where you are going. What I have learned, and am still learning, is that it doesn't matter what happens to you. What does matter is how you handle it.

Life is difficult and full of challenges...

"Either you are in a storm, coming out of a storm, or heading for a storm." And...

BONUS FROM JONAS
"You can't get out of life alive."

So I encourage you not to rust out, but to wear out. And when death catches you, you want to be on your way up.

BONUS FROM JONAS
"I'm on my way to the top and I cannot be stopped!"

Join me with that same, positive attitude. In fact, repeat what I just said:

"I'm on my way to the top and I cannot be stopped!"

BONUS FROM JONAS
"How to turn stumbling blocks into stepping stones, obstacles into opportunities, and pitfalls into promises again…"
All of this starts with a proper attitude.

Attitude

"The longer I live, the more I realize the impact of attitude on life. Attitude, to me, is more important than facts. It is more important than the past, than education, than money, than circumstances, than failures, than success, than what other people think or say or do. It is more important than appearance, giftedness, or skill. It will make or break a company…a church…a home. The remarkable thing is we have a choice every day regarding the attitude we will embrace for that day. We cannot change our past…we cannot change the fact that people will act in a certain way.

"We cannot change the inevitable. The only thing we can do is play on the one string we have, and that is our attitude…I am convinced life is 10% of what happens to me and 90% how I react to it. And, so it is with you…we are in charge of our attitudes."—Charles Swindoll

The Carnegie Institute and Stanford University did a study on 3,000 executives around the world. They were asked, "To what do you attribute your success?" Eighty-five percent said they attributed their success to their attitude; 15 percent attributed their success to their aptitude.

Mr. Jesse Owens was the first African-American athlete to win four gold medals when he competed in track and field during the World Olympics held in Berlin, Germany, in 1936. Mr. Adolph Hitler was ruling Germany and he believed that the Germans were the superior race. His ultimate goal was to rule the world. One of the ways he was planning to demonstrate that the Germans were superior was during the World Olympics by having all of the German athletes to annihilate all of the competitors from around the world and to win gold medals in every area. But Mr. Jesse Owens shattered that false and distorted belief system and philosophy. He taught us the power of the human spirit and demonstrated the discipline, courage, tenacity, focus, and commitment needed when he won against tremendous odds in a hostile environment. He was considered the hero of the 1936 Olympics.

Mr. Owens once said, "Every day will be a learning experience. You will miss more than you catch. Things will change fast. Change with them. Develop an attitude for the future. Don't exist on what you have done exist on what you can do."

BONUS FROM JONAS
"If you perform at your best, even when the situation that you perform in is the worst, you will win!"

Ms. Wilma Rudolph was from a poor black family with 17 children living in the deep South when segregation was the norm. At the age of four, her left leg was crippled by polio. Doctors said that she would always wear a leg brace in order to walk. She refused to believe it. She took off the leg brace when she was twelve and never used it again. Wilma also got off of the sidelines and got into the game.

Before long, she was the fastest sprinter on the Tennessee track team.

It was reported that Wilma said, "The doctors told me that I would never walk again. My mother told me that I would and I believed my mother."

Wilma not only learned to walk, but she ran right into the 1960 Olympics and she won three gold medals in one day. In fact, she was named the fastest woman in the world at that time. She had an "I can do" attitude...and she did it.

Mr. Nelson Mandela fought against apartheid and the injustices done against him and black people in the great country of South Africa. He spent 27 years in prison. He refused to accept and agree to the system of apartheid that treated one group of people inferior and the other superior.

There were times he was encouraged to compromise his beliefs and to weaken his stand against the injustices done to black people in South Africa. If he had given in to the leaders of apartheid, he was promised to be freed from prison earlier. Yet, he refused.

Nelson Mandela was released from prison on February 11, 1990, and later he was elected the first Black African president of South Africa, taking office on May 10, 1994. (6) He forgave those who persecuted him and selected some of the whites to work in his cabinet in order to build a new South Africa and to end apartheid.

"I have cherished the ideal of a free society in which all persons live together in harmony and equal opportunities. It is an ideal which I hope to live for...But if need be, it is an ideal for which I am prepared to die."
—Nelson Mandela, former president of South Africa

Many of you know about Venus and Serena Williams, two of the best women tennis players to ever play the game. Their skills and athletic abilities are awesome. However, my focus is on Mr. Richard Williams, their father, who wanted a better life for his children. Mr. Williams had tenacity and an undeniable, unstoppable, positive attitude. He taught himself the game of tennis through reading books, watching films/videos, and practicing. He had little formal education and grew up in poverty. Mr. Williams had experienced segregation and racism in its most devastating form. But he did not allow that to stop him. Now everyone knows who his daughters are. But it started with him because he did not give up. Even though you are one person, you can still make a positive, powerful, and purposeful difference in the world.

We all have that same kind of resilient spirit in us and it is time to wake it up.

Mother Theresa demonstrated "the power of one." I think about Mother Theresa and the positive contribution that she made to humanity, specifically in Calcutta, India. She demonstrated the unconditional love that we talked about earlier in the book. She believed that no one should die alone. She exemplified a caring attitude. I believe she understood that people don't care how much you know until they know how much you care.

This reminds me of a story of a man who wanted to change the world.

Changing the World

"When I was a young man, I wanted to change the world. I found it was difficult to change the world, so I tried to change my nation. When I found I couldn't change the nation, I began to focus on my town. I couldn't change the town and as an older man, I tried to change my family. Now, as an old man, I realize the only thing I can change is me, and suddenly I realize that if long ago I had changed myself, I could have made an impact on my family. My family and I could have made an impact on our town. Their impact could have changed the nation and I could have indeed changed the world."
—unknown Monk 1110 A.D.

Change your attitude and you can change your world!

Change your attitude, transform your mind and positively impact the world!

Mr. William James said, "The greatest discovery of my generation is that human beings can alter their lives by altering their attitudes of mind."

As I said earlier in the book, in order to be successful, "You need a check up from the neck up."

From the neck down, about the best that you can do is from $300 to $1,000 per week, depending on your ability. From the neck up you are unlimited!

Philippians 4:8 states, "...Whatsoever things are true, whatsoever things are honest, whatsoever things are just, whatsoever things are pure, whatsoever things are lovely, whatsoever things are of good report; if there be any virtue, and if there be any praise, think on these things."

Your thinking controls your mind and your mind dominates your members, because where your mind goes, your members will follow. Again, this ties directly to your attitude.

BONUS FROM JONAS
"Every day above ground is a great day.
If you don't believe it, you just missed one of them.
It's a great day!"

The Storms of Life:

"The Greatest Storm is followed by the Greatest Calm!"

On September 11, 2001, America experienced a horrific attack on New York City's World Trade Center, the Pentagon in Washington, DC and the aborted attack in Pennsylvania.

Approximately three thousand innocent Americans died; leaving thousands more loved ones behind. As a result, America went into a war against Iraq and now with Afghanistan. In these two raging wars, it was reported that 5,356 American soldiers have lost their lives and thousands others have been injured. (7)

I remember two times in my life when I cried publicly; once, when President John F. Kennedy was assassinated and then on that fateful September day. I felt like so many other Americans, down, depressed, shocked, and angry. I prayed for those who lost loved ones and for our country that we would not allow the terrorists to paralyze us and stop us from living our dreams, our goals, and our aspirations. However, many Americans talked about "911" and most of their comments referred to other people. Some even attempted to make biblical references to explain the horrible thing that happened to all of us in America that day.

But after much talking, listening to the news, praying, crying, and just pondering, here's the message that I got out of that terrible experience and I will share it with you. "911" as you well know stands for "emergency, urgency." It carries the thought that it is time to get up and get going and to handle whatever the challenge may be. So here is what I have learned: Time is running out. Whatever you or I plan to do positive with our lives, we must do it now.

BONUS FROM JONAS
"It's Now O'Clock!"

We must...write that book, sing that song, start that business, get that degree, go back to school, get married.

Whatever our dreams are.

Do it now.

Don't die with your music still in you!

I was born on September 13, 1953. Right now, we have the month that I was born, the day that I was born, and the year. After that, there is a dash between the day that I was born and eventually the day that I will die.

In the meantime, I am working very hard on my dash to write this book as part of my dash in order to touch your life as part of my dash. To travel all over the world to make a positive impact by speaking. To have my messages translated into other languages and to present seminars and work-shops. To be interviewed on radio, television, and internet programs...To create programs, books, tapes, CDs, DVDs, and other products as part of my dash. To help young people realize that "they make up 28% of our population but that they are 100% of our future." (8) This is part of my dash.

To have taken care of my mother who died on February 21, 2008, at 84 years old, who took care of me, is part of my dash. To be a great and Godly father is a part of my dash. To live a Christian life is a part of my dash. What is your dash? Why are you here? What are you doing? What is your music? Why aren't you playing it? What is your excuse? Maybe it is "I'm not in the right family." Or "I'm too young...too old. I'm too fat...too skinny. I don't have the right education. Maybe it is the pigment of my skin...my ethnicity...Or I don't live in the right neighborhood...I don't know the right people. Whatever your excuse is, think about 911. It is *your* time. Let go of what is stopping you and live *your* dash.

BONUS FROM JONAS
"Live every day like it is your last day because one of these days, you are going to be right!"

After September 11, 2001, part of the Statue of Liberty was closed because of safety concerns. When tourists visited, they were no longer able to go up into the crown, which is the highest point, offering a panoramic view of New York City and surrounding areas.

How often have you shut down your highest point and made it inaccessible to yourself and to others by not utilizing your full potential? Where nobody could get in. And for how long? Lady Liberty's crown was closed for eight long years.

How long are you going to be closed and inaccessible? Are you going through a renovation, a renewal, a re-assessment so that you can better use what God has given you to be great? Only after being closed down for renovation for awhile can you come out a new creature. You must reinvent yourself. Having invested in yourself, you must recreate yourself; renew, rebuild, restore, and return to your purpose that has been placed in you. Move up to the highest point in your life!

BONUS FROM JONAS
"Some people spend too much time in the basement of their lives instead of going up to the balcony!"

You think down, look down, start talking down, walking down, acting down, and if you aren't careful, you'll be down and you'll die in the basement. Your psychology and your physiology must work together in harmony to produce a positive and a productive life. Your physiology is just as important as your psychology. Come on out of the basement; you can see more and then you can work to achieve more... Move on up to the penthouse. Right now people are in the basement of their lives. They are in a depression.

Your physiology and psychology must change. It starts from the inside out and not the outside in. You want to be flexible and not rigid.

The tourists are limited in how far they can go up into the Statue of Liberty. Lady Liberty's crown, the highest place, has a limit in the number of tourists who can be in it at one time. The restrictions on Lady Liberty and her crown were established by outside forces: Other people. Many people have restricted themselves on how high they can go in their lives to achieve their liberty. No one restricted them. It was not an external force but an internal force. They restricted themselves. They have prevented themselves from access to their purpose. In your crown (your highest place) is where you must live your purpose. Have you restricted yourself? Have you stopped yourself from living and getting your crown? When you refuse to go back and get in your crown, then you are not living what you were made for. You are outside of your purpose. If you have done this, its time now to *start* anew.

You have limited yourself in how high you can go, how

far you can grow, and how bright you can glow. You need to realize that your life needs to be opened up again. You need to have a larger vision of what you can be and what you can do and what you can have.

Sometimes you can be held back, restricted and limited to where you can go from outside forces. Limitations can be imposed on you by others. But often the greatest limits that you face you have placed on yourself. You are blocking yourself from going to the "Crown Level" in your life. No one is doing it to you. You are doing it to yourself.

If you want to get to the crown then you must have a "check up from the neck up."

You may have closed up your own "Liberties" and locked yourself out. You were made to be unlimited.

BONUS FROM JONAS
"In order to get to the top you must first get off of your bottom!"

Our new president, Mr. Barack Obama had the crown on Lady Liberty's head re-opened on July 4th, 2009, the 233rd birthday of the United States of America. What a great symbol of freedom and victory on the anniversary of American Independence.

How many of you have been closed for 5, 10, 15, 20, 25 years? It is time to re-open.

I know that we live in the greatest country in the world. And sometimes we think that freedom is an entitlement with being an American. That we deserve "life, liberty, and the pursuit of happiness." Millions of men and women have given their lives so that we can benefit from the freedom that some of us take for granted. How do we get Americans to unveil our creativity, responsibility? We must make a decision to unveil our greatness.

Celebrate our freedom by embracing our responsibility and accountability. I like what President John F. Kennedy once said: "Ask not what your country can do for you. Ask what you can do for your country."

BONUS FROM JONAS
"Responsibility without accountability is a liability!"

Lady Liberty is a symbol of freedom and the opportunity for "life, liberty and the pursuit of happiness." Just as the crown was closed, preventing visitors, tourists, to go up to the highest place to get the greatest view, there is a direct correlation with Lady Liberty and the Eagle. The eagle represents freedom, responsibility, and accountability. He is the only bird who can fly at the highest altitude and fly higher than any other bird in the sky. In accepting his responsibility he flies to his crown as he pursues his full potential. We too as human beings must fly to our highest heights and take responsibility to live our full potential by living our purpose. After that we each must hold ourselves to a positive standard of accountability.

BONUS FROM JONAS
"In order to achieve greatness, responsibility and accountability have to work on the same team. They must dress in the same uniform. They work together to serve the same purpose!"

The eagle is the king of the air! We are designed to be as eagles and encounter storms as they do. As human beings, however, some of us behave like the other birds and not like the eagle. When the storm comes other birds work to fly against the storm and do not have the strength or stamina to beat it. They start bailing out and heading south! And some birds make the tragic mistake to think that they can out fly the storm.

On the other hand, eagles welcome the storm: They use the wind as an updraft and the storm becomes the wind beneath their wings. Eagles use the storm to their advantage and they are delivered versus allowing the storm to bring destruction to them! As human beings, if we don't prepare for our storms, trying to out-fly, or out-drive, out-maneuver the storm only brings devastation and destruction to our lives.

An eagle flies. He glides, he doesn't flap. An eagle soars. You can't flap your way to greatness. You've got to fly your way to greatness! We weren't called to mount up like a chicken, like a duck or like a turkey. We were called to mount up like an eagle. It is time to summon that eagle spirit that is in You.

All of us have the greatness, eagle spirit in us. It was put in us in advance. Sometimes we look for everything outside of ourselves. People might do things out there. What really matters is what is going on within you. You don't want to react. You want to respond. An eagle responds to the storms of life. Other birds react to it.

BONUS FROM JONAS
"Greatness is never given. It must be developed. It must be fought for!"

"What lies behind us, and what lies in front of us pales in significance to what lies within us!"
—Ralph Waldo Emerson

It's not external. It's internal.

When we are dealing in tough economic times like we are now, we must prepare ourselves. We must winterize ourselves. That's what the eagle does. He winterizes himself. It has been said that the eagle is the only bird that doesn't fly south during the winter. He prepares himself for the storm that is coming. What he is doing is preparing himself to win. He is setting himself up for success. He is working to get a home field advantage. He is working on himself. He is anticipating the storm. I acknowledge that there is a place and a time that we all must be independent. An eagle is independent. This is what the eagle does when he insulates himself and prepares for the storm. What he does is insulate himself not isolate himself. He takes off all of the debris, all of the stuff that is holding him back, that no longer works. Like the eagle, we must take off the things that are impeding our progress. Limits that we have placed on ourselves or have allowed others to place on us.

BONUS FROM JONAS
"People label you so they can limit you!"

We must shed off poison people. Human vampires that will suck all of the life out of you— your dreams, your goals, and your aspirations—and leave you to die and they go to find someone else to suck on.

You must develop the mindset that "sucking days are over."

You must rid your life of dream busters. Like the eagle, we need to work on ourselves now. In order to mount up we must have prepared ourselves for the challenge. Like the eagle, we must focus on what we CAN do and do it relentlessly. If we lack the skills to succeed, then we must go back to school. The focus is on what we can do. Are we doing what is essential, positive and powerful so that we can mount up to win?

BONUS FROM JONAS
"Can't has died! I know he has because I killed him!"

As I mentioned earlier in the book, you need to move from "I can't do avenue" over to **"I CAN do boulevard."** Can we do this? Yes, we can!

My book *How To Fly Like An Eagle With Wings Like A Wimp!* gives you "the education, inspiration and motivation" to help you mount up so that you can "Fly Like An Eagle...!"

Since 911, The Storms Keep on Coming...

BONUS FROM JONAS
"You are either in a storm, coming out of a storm, or heading for a storm."

As Americans, we have encountered many storms. Have *you* been in the storm too long?

According to *USA Today,* the year 2005 came to be known as "The Year of Adversity." The storms came and went: Katrina, Rita, and Wilma, and other disasters. According to the weather people, they had so many storms that the year 2005 was the first time in 62 years where they ran out of letters of the alphabet and had to start over at "A." In 2005 the record number of storms was 27, which surpassed the previous record of 21 storms in 1933. The deadliest storm/ hurricane was Katrina, in 2005, with about 1,800 lives lost. (9)

When we were just working to overcome the physical storms of life that hit America, we were immediately hit by an economic storm. And finally it was announced in December 2008 that Americans had been in a recession for nine months. The storms keep on coming. Approximately 2 million Americans lost their jobs in 2008. Between 2008 and 2010, it is estimated that Americans have lost 14.9 million jobs. As of February 2010, the unemployment rate was 9.7 percent nationwide. It had gone as high as 10 percent nationwide in December 2009, 2 percent above what economists had predicted. This is the highest unemployment rate since 1983. (10)

Everybody has been affected, from Wall Street to Main Street to My Street to Your Street. The stock market, the banks, and the financial services companies were at the core of the economic downturn; Lehman Brothers went belly up; Merrill Lynch was rescued by Bank of America; AIG Insurance Company got a lot of bail out money with no conditions. Ford Motor Company, the maker of the first automobile in America declared bankruptcy; Chrysler was bought out. Whole industries have been seeking government bailouts. Then Bernard Madoff made off with billions of dollars of investors' money who had put all of their faith and trust in him. He had been held to little accountability until $50 billion later, and he was finally sentenced to prison.

The recession has affected many Americans in such a negative way that some are experiencing depression. I know that we are supposed to be in a recession but I decided not to participate.

BONUS FROM JONAS
"Recession is my time for possession."

And it can be your time also if you apply these tested and proven techniques that I share with you in this book! The Old America—with the mindset, "Get a good education, get a job and you are set for life"—the "from the cradle to grave" mentality—those days are gone forever! We had our trust in all of these systems. Everyone has lost something! But in spite of these storms...

BONUS FROM JONAS
"There's no defense against greatness! If there's a crack, then greatness will seep through...If there is no crack, then greatness will break through!
Don't have a breakdown when you are next in line for a positive break through!"

Here is *your* new stimulus plan:

BONUS FROM JONAS
"Don't focus on what you have lost, focus on what you have left, because what you have left is enough to get the job done!"

As I said earlier, some are to blame, but we all are responsible. This is a new day. This is a new time. This is a new opportunity. In the Chinese and Japanese languages, there is no such word as "crisis." Instead, the word is "opportunity."

The future belongs to those who prepare themselves for it. Are you prepared? If not, now is the time. Opportunities are all around you. And if you don't find one—Congratulations! You get the unique privilege and responsibility to create one.

I'm not going to look for someone to bail me out. I may need a hand up but not a hand out. Sometimes, the only help that you'll get is at the end of both of your sleeves. Roll up your sleeves, use both hands, get up and go to work. There's no help coming to rescue you. You must decide to get up and get going. Stop thinking about instant gratification.

BONUS FROM JONAS
"Adversity Is God's University!"

Don't take credit just because they offer it: When you pay minimum then credit card companies benefit maximum. The Scriptures tell us that God will supply all our needs. It never said, He will supply our greed. Make sure that you pay off whatever that bill is within the 30-day period instead of allowing it to accumulate with a large amount of interest. A lot of things are charged on a credit card that shouldn't be. A Happy Meal is charged on a credit card.

That meal cost $5, but if not paid off within 30 days, then you could be spending $35 on a meal you ate 25 years ago.

In fact, I believe in the "cash and carry" method. If you don't have the cash, then you don't carry it. Or use layaway. You save for it, pay a little on it, then at the end when you have paid for it in full, you take the product home. No interest charged.

There are storms and we have experienced storms. The economy is a storm. A bad relationship is a storm. Not having a job is a storm. Having health challenges is a storm. Not having adequate health care is a storm. Having more month at the end of your money is a storm. I don't know what kind of storm that you are in or the kind of storm that you are facing right now. You must develop a positive attitude followed with positive action, believing, "Yes, I can. You are talking to me about the power of positive thinking? Having a positive attitude? That is hard!" You are right; it is hard! That is why I find this poem so meaningful. And I believe that it can help you too.

Sometimes
"If times are hard, and you feel blue
Think of others, worrying too;
Just because your trials are many,
Do not think the rest of us haven't any.
Life is made up of smiles and tears,
Joys and sorrow, mixed with fears;
And though to us it seems one-sided
Trouble is pretty well divided.
If we could look in every heart,
We will find that each one has, his part
And those who travel fortune's road
Sometimes carry the biggest load."
—Unknown

Where are you in life right now? And what is it that you are dealing with? Whether you are dealing with fear, or whether it is worry, or with hard times this is the time to take your rightful place. Wherever you are, that's the place to start. Wherever you are in life, start now to invest in yourself and your future.

BONUS FROM JONAS
"The biggest room in the whole-wide world is room for improvement. You can always better your best."

What are you doing to make a positive difference where you are? I challenge you to bloom where you are planted. Are you making a dent, or are you making a positive difference? When you are into the dent lifestyle you are just pointing out what is obvious. But when you are with the positive difference mentality, you are taking on your responsibility and taking your rightful place, living your purpose with a passion. In other words, you are taking a stand against some things. What are you against and what are you for?

BONUS FROM JONAS
"If you don't stand for something, you'll fall for anything."

You will develop the attitude of, "I will never give up, never give in and never give out. It is always too early to quit, because a quitter never wins and a winner never quits."

I also believe that the only times that you should sing the blues, long-term, is when you are getting paid for it. If you are not...forget it. Either you are part of the situation/problem, or you are part of the solution. I have decided in light of all of the challenges that are going on in this country and world that I am going to be a part of the solution. And people don't care about the storms that you have encountered.

All they want to know is "Did you bring the ship in?"

Together we can bring the ship in and make it a better world. We need more positive, action-oriented people who will help make the world a better place. You cannot control the winds in life but you can and *must* adjust your sails. You are waiting for your ship to come in...but you are at the airport. Ships don't come in at the airport. Make sure that you have sent a ship out for it to come in. You must be at the harbor to meet your ship.

Sometimes we are at the wrong place at the wrong time. Where are you in your life? Educationally, spiritually, emotionally, intellectually, relationally, physically, geographically, and financially?

And are those the places that you are supposed to be? This is dealing with human self-assessment.

Take a look at the man, at the woman, at the boy, at the girl in the mirror.

You might say, how could I make it a better world? I am only one person.

You are right. But the first point I would like to share with you is this: Your world is wherever you are. The second major point is that the majority of people have never made a positive impact at the beginning of any worthwhile cause. It has always been the minority. Allow me to give a few quick examples. Rosa Parks refused to give up her seat. The day she sat down, the world stood up. Dr. Martin Luther King, Jr., during the Civil Rights Movement led approximately 250,000 people in the March on Washington August 28, 1963, fighting for jobs and freedom. As a result, Congress passed the Civil Rights Act in 1964, which banned racial discrimination in public places, in public education and enforced the right to vote for all Americans. (11)

Dr. King gave his famous, "I Have A Dream" speech, which today still echoes in people's minds around the world.

Mahatma Gandhi took a stand against oppression for the people of India.

Susan B. Anthony fought for women to have the right to vote. In a spiritual sense, think about Moses and how God used him to deliver his people from Egyptian bondage. Moses led approximately 2 million people out of Egypt. When you read about Jesus, He took 12 disciples and used them in turning a world that was upside down right side up. The point that I am making is that you, too, can and must make your positive impact on humanity.

BONUS FROM JONAS
**"Instead of saying I am only one say
after me with enthusiasm,
"I am *the one*...Because, although I am living in tough
times, I have been chosen for such a time as this!"**

This reflects back to the story that I shared earlier about changing your world.

It starts with me having a positive attitude, which must be followed with positive action. Transformation begins with me. There can never be any *we* until I have taken care of *me*. We are not talking about being selfish; we are talking about doing what is essential within each of us *first*.

If I want to make a positive impact in the world, I must first change me. Then in turn, I can change my family, my family and I work to change the community, then we work together to change our nation, and ultimately we work together to change the world. You have to choose to be a positive person with a positive attitude and positive action.

It is *your* choice. "It's not about we right now, but its about me. It's me! It's me! It's me, oh Lord."

BONUS FROM JONAS
"The man who is rowing his boat doesn't have time to rock it!"

We have now covered positive attitude coupled with positive action.

Aptitude

"When the student is ready, the teacher will appear."

We just talked about the importance of having a positive attitude. As we indicated earlier with the two studies we shared, 85 percent of success is attributed to attitude. The other 15 percent is aptitude. That is what we are going to focus on now.

With an "I can do" attitude and a "No, I can't" aptitude, you are all dressed up with no place to go. I want you to be able to go for your goals.

BONUS FROM JONAS
"It's what you learn after you know it all that makes a positive difference!"

Garden Story

You have heard it said that the grass is always greener on the other side. Have you turned over grass lately? Well, if you have then you would discover that it is brown. But yours could be greener if you are willing to water it, and give it the proper nutrients and fertilizer that it needs to grow.

You also have to be willing to de-weed it. I have noticed that in the garden of life, you do not have to plant weeds; they grow automatically. Having a positive attitude only is not going to save your garden. You must pull the weeds out. That requires skill.

BONUS FROM JONAS
"A person convinced against his or her own will is of the same opinion still."

This illustration is a metaphor for our lives. In this chapter you will learn how to "take a chance, take charge, and take control of your life."

Take a Chance

In order to take a chance, you have to be willing to go out on a limb...after all that is where all of the fruit is. If you want to do something that you have never done before, then you have to become someone whom you have never been before. When you take a chance you must be willing to move out of your comfort zone. Remove the old mindset. The mindset of "business as usual" or "birds of a feather flock together."

And take a chance on *you!*

Many people are willing to go to Atlantic City, Las Vegas, and Reno to gamble. They are willing to take a chance on a one-armed bandit and play slot machines. However, they are not willing to take a chance on themselves. I am writing to you to encourage you to invest in *you.* It may require that you go back to school to get your GED, associate degree, bachelor degree, masters degree, or even your PhD or other professional credentials. But you must be willing to do it. You might have to read more books, go to more seminars, take more classes, listen to more CDs or cassettes, and watch more DVDs or videos. Be willing to do whatever is right to get what you want.

The average American only reads one book per year. If you would read one book per month in the areas of your expertise, in five years you would have read sixty books when the average American would have only read five.

Don't you think that would give you a competitive advantage in the global marketplace? Yes, it will. What I have learned is that reading autobiographies of people who have done what you want to do can help you tremendously. They will tell you about their struggles and their triumphs. I also have learned that I am not going to live long enough to make all of the mistakes myself. Learning from other people's experiences is critical.

Someone once said, "Well, I want to learn from my own experiences." I also used to think like that. However, what I discovered is that I would rather be taught by other people's experiences versus my own. Learning from others' mistakes is a better way to learn. Some people really believe that experience is the best teacher. But experience tests you first and teaches you second. You want to be taught first and tested second.

Because "lessons are repeated until learned."

BONUS FROM JONAS
"There is a shortcut to education.
Find out who knows the answer and ask them!"

As I said earlier, there are three kinds of people in this world.

BONUS FROM JONAS
"Those who make things happen;
they are assertive. Those who watch things happen;
they are passive. And those who wonder what happened; they are aggressive."

What kind of a person are you?
Are you passive, aggressive, or assertive?

Passive People
There are some people who do not take a chance on themselves because they are passive. They allow other people to walk all over them. Of course; why not? They have a welcome mat on their chest. They are lying down on the pathway of life and they have the nerve to get upset because people are wiping their feet on and disrespecting them.

68

Don't you think it is time to get up from down there, with the attitude of "enough is enough"? Sometimes I ask people, "How are you doing today?" They respond to me, "I'm doing fine under the circumstances." I always ask them, "What are you doing down there under the circumstances? We were designed to rise above our circumstances."

Aggressive People

Some people are letting life and circumstances walk all over them. However, others are aggressive and walk all over other people. Aggressive people have the bulldozer mentality and violate the rights of other people. A bulldozer's function is to run over other things. They don't care about anyone else. "It's my way, or the highway."

They are all about "me." In a sense they are dream breakers, in this case, they break you and your dreams.

Assertive People

Assertive people work to live their dreams and will not let anyone stop them. However, they will not do anything to prevent others from living their dreams. Assertive people take care of their own dreams and they are willing to help others. They will not allow themselves to be violated and will not violate the rights of others. They know exactly what they want if they go to a seminar, workshop, conference, or even in a relationship. They know what they are going in there for and they do not come out without it. They work to create a situation where everyone wins. Again I ask you, "What kind of person are you: passive, aggressive, or assertive?"

Take Charge

When you take charge you are accepting responsibility for who you are and for where you are. You realize that in life, most of the time, all of the help that you will ever get is at the end of both of your sleeves. You need to roll up your sleeves and go to work. Then you will "see and seize every moment." You will not allow anyone, or anything to turn you around. You have the mind-set and the attitude that, "I'm on my way to the top and cannot be stopped."

"Those of us who have struggled across the mountain
have indeed come to a land of milk and honey,
but that is not to say that all is eternally well because
in order to get the milk you must persuade the cow to
give, and in order to get the honey,
you must run the risk of getting stung."—Mr. James
McCuller, Action for a Better Community

You realize that you have hurts, habits, and hang-ups
that you must address. You are willing to...

BONUS FROM JONAS
"Admit it and quit it! You know that if you don't have a test, that you will never have a testimony."

What I have learned is that far too many people are
possessed with only the "moanies" mentality. People are always talking about how bad things are. It's the government.
It's the neighborhood that I live in. It's the old people that
I have to work with everyday. It's my children. It's my wife
(my husband). It's the economy. It's the color of my skin. I'm
too fat (too skinny). This book is designed to help you stop
the "moanies" and start the testimonies.

Go back and get the lessons because none of these things
that you just named are designed to stop you. However, they
are tests to see how serious you are about getting what you
claim that you want. Often times you may see the blisters,
but miss the blessings. And, you must acknowledge that the
only person that you can change is *you.*

"Most people are educated way beyond their level of execution." You have heard that knowledge is power; knowledge
is *not* power. Knowledge is potential power. You can have all
of the knowledge in the world and it will never help you unless
you put it into action. "Some people have more degrees than
a thermometer, but they are not doing anything with them."

Whitney Young said that, "It is better to be prepared for
an opportunity and not have one than to have an opportunity
and not be prepared."

This is *your* opportunity. Some people are waiting for
opportunity to knock. But in reality, opportunity resides in
you. It is fighting to get out and it is knocking. The knocking
is not coming from outside.

The knocking is coming from within. It is knocking and saying, "Let me out!" Your greatness, your potential is knocking and saying, "Let me out!"

BONUS FROM JONAS
"You can either have a breakdown or a *breakthrough*. I recommend you have a *breakthrough!*"

I am here to help you to have a positive breakthrough. Malcolm X said, "Education is our passport to the future, for tomorrow belongs to those who prepare for it today." Abraham Lincoln said, "I will study and prepare myself and someday my time will come." A part of this preparation is to implement what I call the holistic approach to life. One must grow in four areas: spiritually, intellectually, physically, and relationally.

Spiritual
I believe that...

BONUS FROM JONAS
"If you put God first, you'll never come in second."

My prayer for you is: "Beloved, I wish above all things that you may prosper and be in health, even as your soul prospers..." (3rd John 1:2).

Intellectual
It is important to invest in yourself. Reading positive and purposeful books is invaluable. Some people say that education is expensive. Yes, you are right. It is expensive. But have you priced ignorance lately? It costs even more. The United Negro College Fund has a motto: "The mind is a terrible thing to waste." To get to where you need to go, you must build relationships with positive and successful people who can help you to build the skills that you need. Get a coach or a mentor with whom you can work on a one-on-one basis, who can help you to build the skills that you need.

In addition, I recommend listening to "educational, inspirational, and motivational" CDs and cassettes and watching DVDs and videos that will help you to pursue the kind of life that you desire and deserve. Perhaps some might say, "Well, I don't like to read." Or, "I can hardly read." Here is one thing that you can do: Purchase the CD/cassette, or borrow it from the library, push it in the player and the author will read the book to you as you follow along. Only in America! It cannot get any easier than that. Some people are more eager to make excuses for why they can't rather than developing reasons why they can.

I have turned my car into what I call the "University on Wheels" because while driving in my car, I learned some of the things that I am sharing in this book. For example, while driving, I learned how to be a better leader, speaker, and communicator, as well as how to build my vocabulary and have a positive attitude. Maximizing the time spent in my car allows me to de-weed my mind from the negativity that is all around me.

An African Proverb says, "If there's no enemy within the enemy without can do you no harm."

Be Careful
"Be careful of your thoughts
For your thoughts become your words.
Be careful of your words
For your words become your actions.
Be careful of your actions
For your actions become your habits.
Be careful of your habits
For your habits become your character.
Be careful of your character
For your character becomes your destiny."
—Samuel Smiles

To continue to increase your knowledge there are three areas that you need to focus on: (1) Your strengths, (2) becoming a laser learner, and (3) areas needing improvement. Spend 80 percent of your time on your strengths, 15 percent of your time on being a laser learner. And 5 percent needs to be delegated to someone who has the expertise, skills, and competency in that area. If you are not good in that 5 percent area, then hire someone who is. When you delegate that doesn't make you weak; it makes you wise. Dr. Martin Luther King, Jr., captured this point by saying, "If you can't be a pine on top of a hill, be a shrub in the valley, but be the best little shrub on the side of the hill. Be a bush if you can't be a tree. If you can't be a highway, just be a trail. If you can't be the sun, be a star. For it isn't by size that you win or fail. Be the best of whatever you are..."

Physical

You must take time for yourself. Create joy in the journey and not in the destination.

I do not know what it is for you. Maybe it is walking, running, or swimming. Maybe it is lifting weights. Maybe it is taking a relaxing bubble bath, or a hot shower. Whatever it is, take good care of yourself. Refer to the goal section that I talked about earlier and review the importance of being healthy.

Relational

A lot of people do not realize this, but life is all about relationships. Sometimes we focus only on romantic relationships, but again, we are relational beings. "I need you and you need me." We need people, but we do not need any one person in order to succeed in life.

BONUS FROM JONAS
**"I've never met an audience that didn't bring me joy.
Some people bring me joy when they enter the room.
Others bring me joy when they leave the room.
Nevertheless, they bring me joy."**

"Some people come into our lives for a reason, for a season, or for a righteous lifetime." Therefore, it is important to learn more about people to know how to deal with different people and the situations that you are in with them. People skills are essential.

There are three learning styles that you must be aware of, learn, and implement when you are communicating effectively with people: visual, auditory, and kinesthetic. Statistics state that in this country 89 percent of people are visual learners.

Visual Learners

Visual learners learn and feel valued by what they see. For example, to say to a visual learner that "I love you" will not get it. You have to show them by bringing flowers, or taking them out to a nice expensive dinner. Or you bring them candy. It is very important how the package is wrapped. Talk is cheap to the visual learner. Your actions show them how valuable they are to you.

Auditory Learners

You can show the auditory learner all that you want, but they want to *hear* it. They are people who feel important and valued by hearing...the auditory learner. These individuals want to hear, "I love you" through the song and the lyric. They want you to say it and to say it regularly.

Kinesthetic Learners

The kinesthetic learner communicates mostly based upon feelings. You must connect with them emotionally first. They have a tendency sometimes to want to touch you or hug you when they are communicating with you. And they use the word "feelings" in their language.

With all three of these groups you must pay attention to what they say because in listening to them, they will tell you which group they are in most of the time. You will come into contact with people who have all of these different learning styles. Considering and learning these differences will help you to more successfully relate to people around you. For the visual, auditory, and kinesthetic learners, each particular style is dominant, but it doesn't mean that it is the only learning style they use.

Although auditory learners learn predominantly through hearing they use visual (pictures) and kinesthetic (feelings) styles as well. To build rapport with each of these personality learning styles you will be successful when you "match and mirror" them.

You are matching their movements and their words. This indicates that you value them and want to communicate with them where they are.

People Skills Are Powerful

"No one becomes successful or accomplishes anything of lasting significance without effective people skills.

"No matter how ambitious, capable, clear-thinking, competent, decisive, dependable, educated, energetic, responsible, serious, shrewd, sophisticated, wise, and witty you are, if you don't relate well to other people, you won't make it.

"No matter how professionally competent, financially adept, physically solid you are, without an understanding of human nature, a genuine interest in the people around you, and the ability to establish personal bonds with them, you are severely limited in what you can achieve."
—Author Unknown

A study published by the Carnegie Institute of Technology reports that 15 percent of financial and career success is due to technical competence. But 85 percent is due to interpersonal skills. Your ability to be promoted and opportunities for long term financial success hinges to a great degree, on your ability to communicate effectively with people. Human resource professionals estimate that more than 80 percent of the people who fail at their jobs do so for one reason: They don't relate well to other people. Recent studies show that even in highly technical jobs, success or failure is determined more by human relations skills than by technical proficiency.

Mr. Warren Buffet and Mr. Bill Gates, the two wealthiest men in America, were interviewed as part of a symposium at Columbia University business school in New York City in November 2009. Mr. Buffet challenged the students: "If you apply yourself in mastering business skills, I will invest $100,000 in you. But if you master your communication skills, then I will add $500,000 more." In indicating the importance of mastering communication skills, he spoke about the Dale Carnegie course and how it helped him tremendously. Like Mr. Buffet, I emphasize how valuable communication skills are.

I am also a graduate of the Dale Carnegie course. It took me 11 years of being relentless to get in; something always blocked me. Finally, I was selected by Eastman Kodak Company to represent them in the Dale Carnegie Training course and I went and graduated at the top of my class. As a result, I was recruited on two separate occasions to return to help those who worked for Fortune 500 Companies and other professionals in a variety of other industries who were taking the course as well. I was practicing being a laser learner even back then, because I knew what I wanted and I didn't stop until I got it. I didn't give in, I didn't give up and I didn't give out. So I got double for my trouble.

Mr. Zig Ziglar said, "You can have everything in life that you want, if you help enough other people get what they want."

Take Control

When you take control, you accept responsibility for who you are and whose you are.

BONUS FROM JONAS
"You can't change what you do not acknowledge."

You guide your mind and your thoughts and you take positive action. The day you accept full responsibility for all of your actions is the day you start to go to the top. People who take control do not listen to the "naysayers" who tell them what they cannot do.

You also realize and acknowledge that on the sea of life, you cannot control the wind, but you can adjust your sail. So you spend your time focusing on the reasons why you can rather than looking for excuses for why you cannot. It was Mr. Bill Demby who once said, "There are not really enough crutches in the world for all of the lame excuses." What is your compelling reason that will drive you to higher heights? Sometimes well-meaning friends, acquaintances, and even professionals will tell you that you are not college material; that you cannot be an entrepreneur, doctor, lawyer, or an engineer. They might say that you cannot have your own television show, radio program, or internet broadcast. Or that you cannot write your own book because no one in your family has ever done it.

Some might say, "Why don't you just get a job? Learn to work with your hands; you don't have the brain power and the technical skills to make those things a reality." We spoke about these types of people under the heading of dream breakers.

However, I want you to know that you *can* do it. Some of us are from a people who would not give up. We came from a people who had the tenacity and conviction which said, "Freedom, or death. Either I am going to be free, or I am going to die in pursuit of achieving that goal."

Some, when they were caught reading, their eyes were plucked out. When they were caught writing their fingers were cut off. When they diligently worked to learn how to articulate their thoughts, through effective communication, their tongues were mutilated. Yet, they did not allow that to stop them. But of course that did slow them down. I have learned that no one can stop you, but *you*. And I want you to know that in life, you are going to have struggles.

BONUS FROM JONAS
"No struggle, no strength. Strength comes through the struggle."

Mr. Frederick Douglas said, "If there is no struggle, there is no progress."

This story is told about the caterpillar and illustrates the struggles and the strength that occurs when it goes through the process of becoming a butterfly.

The Butterfly Story

In the process of becoming a butterfly, a caterpillar first goes into a cocoon and in this cocoon there is a transformation going on—a metamorphosis, if you will. If anyone tampers with the process, this can be detrimental to the butterfly. One day a little boy saw the cocoon and the struggling butterfly trying to emerge. So he decided to help the butterfly by opening up the cocoon. When he did, the butterfly did come out, but it was deformed, underdeveloped, and weak. The butterfly came out prematurely. Its wings were not fully developed. So the butterfly was not able to fly. It died.

You see, strength comes from the struggle and as the butterfly emerges through the resistance of the cocoon, there is the release of vital chemical energy, if you will. As the butterfly pushes his body through the cocoon, this chemical energy goes through its wings and nourishes and strengthens them, which gives the butterfly the power to fly.

Sometimes in life when we think we are helping something, or someone, in reality we could be hurting them. Most times in life, strength comes through the struggle.

BONUS FROM JONAS
"The caterpillar has a lot of legs.
No matter how fast it runs, it won't fly until
it is transformed into a butterfly."

In taking control of your life, you must make a decision to be transformed into the person that you need to be in order to fly to higher heights.

Mr. George Washington Carver said, "Most people search high and wide for the keys to success; if they only knew that the key to their dreams lies within."

You are the key to your success. As I said before, life is full of distractions.

"It is important to stay focused because Defeat comes from looking back; Distractions come from looking around; Discouragement comes from looking down; but Deliverance comes from looking up." You want to hold fast to what you want, which means you must be willing to grab it. Then hold on. That means you've got it. And hold out, which means you are going to grip it.

You will not accept "no" for an answer. In pursuing my dreams, my goals and my aspirations, some people have told me no. I can't do it.

BONUS FROM JONAS
"When people say 'no' to me,
I add a 'w' and Do It Now!"

Mr. Peter Lowe said, "The most common trait I have found in all successful people is that they have conquered the temptation to give up."

Altitude

Altitude is deciding to utilize all of the skills that you have learned from this book that will enable you to fly to higher heights. This means flying above mediocrity, flying above "I can't do," flying above the status quo, flying above the average, flying above no one in the family ever did that before, flying higher and higher above any and all excuses. Now you are prepared to fly higher because you are "in it to win it."

I like what Mr. Patrick Overton said, "When we walk to the edge of all the light we have and take the step into the darkness of the unknown, we must believe that one of two things will happen. There will be something solid for us to stand on, or we will be taught to fly."

This book is written to teach you how to fly again. The African Proverb I mentioned earlier is appropriate here too: "If there's no enemy within, the enemy without can do you no harm." Use what is in you and the time is now. Because...

"Yesterday is history, tomorrow is a mystery, today is a gift, that's why we call it the present."—Unknown

BONUS FROM JONAS
"Feed your faith and your fear will starve to death."

Of course, as you take off for a higher altitude, it is not going to be a direct flight to your desired destination. At first, you will be off course more times than on.

For example, when I flew down to South Carolina for my mother's 80th birthday, I learned that it is common knowledge in the airline industry that an airplane is off course 90 percent of the time. Also course corrections are constantly being made throughout the flight.

I did arrive safely in South Carolina. This is similar to lifting off toward your dreams. You too will need to make course corrections. While flying on a plane, sometimes you experience turbulence. So make sure you fasten your seat belt.

You also need to fasten your seat belt when you are working to fly to the next level. In addition, remember, just as airline professionals inform us, using the flight analogy, that in the case of an emergency, or a drop in the cabin air pressure, there will be an oxygen mask that will drop in front of you. You would be told to first secure your own mask and then that of your loved ones. You must first secure your own future. Know where you are going. Make sure that you have purchased a ticket, perhaps a one way ticket to your destination. To your dreams. To your future!

I like what Mr. Les Brown, the motivational speaker, said: "Leap and grow wings on your way down." I know that you have heard it is lonely at the top. It is not when you take your loved ones and others with you.

Dr. John Maxwell said that, "If there is faith in the future, there is power in the present." You want to use that power to create the kind of destiny that you desire and deserve. "According to the law of aerodynamics a bumblebee is not supposed to be able to fly, because its body is too large and its wings are too short.

The bumblebee didn't know anything about the law of aerodynamics, nor did he care. He said,"I'm going to fly!" And he did!

I am like that bumblebee. I did not know I was not supposed to be able to do and achieve great things. I just went out and did them. I challenge you to fly above other people's limitations of you and your abilities. "Just keep on flying. Flying above the negativity in the media, in the politicians, above the recession. And remember what I said earlier, that "recession is my time for possession." And it can be for you too.

Flying above the economy, above the unemployment rate, above health care alternatives, above lack of education, above environmental factors…*you* add your own challenge/opportunity here…" Tear up the old script that other people have written for you and start your own. And it starts with, "Once upon a time…"

You must maintain hope for your future and see through eyes like those of Ms. Oprah Winfrey. Oprah said, "When I look into the future, it's so bright it burns my eyes." You are focusing on the future after all, that is where you are going to spend the rest of your life. Now you can apply this…

BONUS FROM JONAS
"My future is so bright I'm going to need sunglasses!"

"You don't have to be great to get started, but you have to get started in order to be *great*."

Chapter Four

Greatness

CONGRATULATIONS! YOU HAVE MADE IT to greatness! It's a new beginning. You have a new canvas and the power to create the kind of life that you desire and you deserve.

In Latin, to educate means "to lead and to draw out." The purpose of this book is to lead and to draw out the greatness in you.

G-Greatness

BONUS FROM JONAS
"Since Greatness Is Possible, Excellence Is Not Enough!
Go For Greatness!"

"Within your veins flows the blood of
ancestors more powerful than ever known.
Within your chest beats the heart of royalty."

To achieve greatness you must first go within in order to manifest it without. Developing the greatness from within. President Barack Obama said, "Greatness is never given; it always must be earned." This chapter is not about focusing on the external. It focuses on the internal *you*. Before you go without you must first go within.

As I stated before, "I don't know about your past, I don't even know about your present, but I do know about your future. It is spotless." Maybe you have lost your zeal.

Maybe you have failed in the past or you are thinking that you can't do it.

BONUS FROM JONAS
"Don't focus on what you have lost...focus on what you have left, because what you have left is enough to get the job done!"

I am not speaking as a psychologist, pediatrician, or sociologist. I am speaking as a committed father and as a professional in the field of human development for more than 30 years. I have worked in corporate America at Xerox Corporation and Eastman Kodak Company, with other Fortune 500 companies, professional organizations, in the business community, with international audiences, in schools and colleges, in churches, and with other community institutions across the country.

BONUS FROM JONAS
"Yes it is True. The seed of greatness Is In You!"

There are three stages that each human being must go through in order to be healthy, happy and whole: (1) dependence, (2) independence, and (3) interdependence. This will help us to learn and to develop ourselves to full maturity. In order to develop the greatness within, you must take a look at your own stages of development so that you can tap into your full potential.

The Dependent Stage: Infant

When we were born we were attached to our mother's umbilical cord. This was the method where we received all of our food and our essential nutrients. Then, once the baby is born, within moments, that umbilical cord is cut. No longer is the baby physically attached to its mother and getting its food through the umbilical cord. The infant is dependent on its parents for food, shelter, clothing, and bathing. There is very little that the baby can do for itself. The baby can't walk or talk. You too were helpless and dependent when you were a baby.

Now, if you want the baby to move to a different location, you as the adult must pick up the baby and take it there. The only method of communicating as an infant is by crying. And this is normal. And it is a healthy stage as long as the baby is getting the nutrients, vitamins, proteins, and minerals so it develops fully to the next stage.

All of this is provided for the baby while it is in the infant/dependent stage.

This stage is a short period of time but very critical in the healthy development of a child. Remember that all of the baby's needs are being taken care of by the mother, father, or another adult.

Toddler

The baby is being given new information on what to do and what not to do, as we prepare it to move from the infant stage to the toddler stage. During the toddler stage they are being taught the difference between right and wrong. They are learning how to walk, how to talk, how to behave, and how to use the potty/bathroom. And they are still depending on their parents or other adults for all of their needs. Parents are preparing them for the next stage. Homes with toddlers in them must be childproofed.

One of the reasons we childproof our home is because toddlers will explore using their hands and their mouths. We must restrict them to certain areas so that they have a safe environment. Parents are responsible to protect their toddlers from hurting themselves or others. By the time the child is two years old, he or she is learning how to walk and talk and to have their way.

What was normal is now abnormal because they stayed in that stage too long. They are supposed to move from infant to toddler to adolescent to adult. That is the normal progression for healthy growth and maturity. Psychologists indicate that the first five years of life are the formative years. When there is a breakdown in the teaching and development of a child during this stage, it produces a malnourished, deformed unhealthy person. Whether physically, mentally, emotionally, or spiritually. If they aren't taught right, they become a liability to society right at this stage. Right *here*: At the toddler stage.

The potential doctors, lawyers, business leaders, preachers, and teachers, are lost right here. When this shows up in adulthood, it is nothing new. If you abdicate your teaching responsibility as a parent here, you develop a menace to society instead of developing a minister. You failed to do your job. Now in the infant and toddler stages there is major dependence on the mother and father and other adults who play a critical role in the growth and development of the child. Now we come to the adolescent stage.

Adolescent

Let them tell it. They know more than everybody else. More than the father, more than the mother, more than the teacher, more than the preacher, more than the police officer; even more than God. However, they can feed themselves, dress themselves, groom themselves and they have responsibilities. While still in high school, they are supposed to be developing good study habits, doing their homework, making good grades, and completing household chores. But they are looking to re-attach the umbilical cord that was cut at birth. This is abnormal. These children are growing out but not growing up. The biggest thing about them is their appetite. They want to play computer games and to party. They don't want rules or regulations.

They want to be grown but they refuse to do what it takes to be grown. They drink up all the milk and put the carton back in the refrigerator. Empty!

When the adolescent is being rebellious and disrespectful, the parents must confront the child, make him or her aware of the breach, deal with the issue, come up with a solution and then the adolescent must execute with precision. Because of the adolescent's "know-it-all" attitude, the parents must re-teach them the value of listening, obeying and remaining teachable.

The Independent Stage: Adult Conduct and Character

When we arrive at this stage we are supposed to be independent and healthy.

We are supposed to be...

BONUS FROM JONAS
"Grown and gone!"

None of these stages of development were designed to have us get stuck or to stop there. It is an active process of human development. Each stage is a progression toward becoming a healthy and mature person. After I had graduated from high school, I went back to visit my elementary classroom. I was amazed at the size of the seats (chair and desk) that I used to sit in. I remember so vividly when I was sitting in those seats. They seemed to be so big, then. The chair was designed for me when I was in third grade. If I returned 10 years later and could still fit in that little chair with its attached desk, then something was wrong. Abnormal. The chair didn't fit anymore because I was grown. Just as I no longer fit in the chair in the 3rd grade class, it is the same once you are "grown and gone." At this stage, you have completed college, gotten a job, and now you are making a six-figure income. You are providing for your own food, clothing, shelter, and education.

Now you are ready to leave and to cleave, to get married and to create your own family.

When you are making a six-figure income, you don't ride off into the sunset. It is reciprocal: There may come a time when mothers and fathers will need you. This is a reciprocal relationship. They may be sick and weak and going back to the infant and toddler stages. You have to feed them, clothe them, cook for them and care for them. And if you grew up right. It is an automatic choice. They may have made mistakes. They didn't abort you, they didn't give you strychnine to drink instead of milk. When you are "grown and gone," it is your responsibility to do what is necessary to grow. You gladly invest in yourself because you are taking responsibility for your life and you understand that you are worth it. Your employer does not have the responsibility to take care of you from the cradle to the grave. After your parents, you should be able to say, "By the help of God, I can take it from here."

On the other hand, when a person does not go through developmental stages in a healthy or proper way, they seek to go back and to re-attach themselves to their mother's umbilical cord which is not normal. This is not a viable option. The umbilical cord has been cut permanently and forever. But they are seeking to re-attach emotionally, psychologically and mentally. Sometimes you can't fix it. Sometimes, you cannot recapture what you have lost, but you can grow with what you have left.

BONUS FROM JONAS
"If you want to do something that you have never done before, then you have to become the person that you have never been before!"

You cannot use the same level of conversation and conduct that got you here to develop the kind of character that you must continue to develop in order to be Great.

These individuals are now trying to move back home when they are supposed to be "grown and gone."

BONUS FROM JONAS
"When you are green, you are growing...when you are ripe and not plucked to do something positive, and you stay on the vine, the next stage after being ripe is being rotten!"

Your goal is to stay in the stage of green and growing. Not ripe and rotten. Cut the umbilical cord so you can make an indelible mark on humanity. When you stay in any of these stages longer than you were supposed to then that stunts your growth, spiritually, physically, psychologically, emotionally and intellectually. Now let's go to the stage of interdependence.

Adult Interdependence

BONUS FROM JONAS
"Growing old is mandatory but growing up is a decision!"

I need you and you need me. But most have not made the transformation. You can't achieve greatness and stay in the adolescent stage. Life is a positive and active progression. You never come to a place where you stay. You are always growing.

Each stage has its purposeful and rightful place. It is food for your faith but you must go through all of these stages in a healthy way.

BONUS FROM JONAS
"Nourish yourself so you can flourish!"

Food for your faith helps you to be faithful to your purpose. Healthy food feeds your faith. Now you are demonstrating that success leaves successors. And you move from success to significance.

No longer are you living the three Ps: pouting, pondering, and punching. Without dealing with developmental stages properly, we will have psychological, emotional, and spiritual deficiencies: "Hurting people hurt people."

BONUS FROM JONAS
"Most people in America don't have ulcers because of what they are eating. Most people in America have ulcers because of what is eating them: unresolved issues."

We want to feel good without being good. We want to numb out and forge ahead. The scripture says that "My people are destroyed because of lack of knowledge..." (Hosea 4:6). When you go through all three of these stages, it is normal, necessary, and natural now you are ready to take your life back.

Now that we have covered the three stages of development, where are you? Make an assessment and look at your dependence, your independence and your interdependence.

BONUS FROM JONAS
"Its time to stop whining and start shining!"

BONUS FROM JONAS
"Don't allow your abilities to take you a place where your character cannot keep you!"

You have done a lot of hard work and made a lot of sacrifices to get the education and accomplishments that you are now enjoying. Congratulations! Greatness requires of you a greater level of commitment, sacrifice, and focus than what you have ever put forth before.

BONUS FROM JONAS
"Champions are not developed in the ring. Champions are developed in practice and revealed in the ring!"

Building a great life, a great relationship, and a great business all starts with positive practice first and that helps you to develop a greater *you.*

You need to go through resistance training: Learn not to go with the flow. Be willing to swim against the current and make a positive difference. This gives you the stamina, skills and strength to bring your dreams to fruition. As I said earlier...

BONUS FROM JONAS
"Don't go where the path may lead, but go where there is no path and leave a trail."

I believe that each one of you has what it takes to be a trailblazer!

BONUS FROM JONAS
"Yes it is true, the seed of greatness is in *you!*"

Recognize and acknowledge that you are special, that you are biologically unique and there is not another person on this planet like you.

BONUS FROM JONAS
**"No one else can duplicate your handwriting, your fingerprints, your voice and, of course, when you get married, no one can duplicate your child. I want you to know that you were born an original.
Don't you dare die a copy!"**

Be the best that you can be.

Develop the mental toughness and the positive statement that, "I am only one, but I am the *one*. I cannot do everything, but I can do something; And, what I should do and can do, by the grace of God, I will do."

I like what Dr. Martin Luther King, Jr. said about greatness:

"Everybody can be great because everybody can serve. You don't have to have a college degree to serve. You don't have to make your subject and your verb agree to serve. You don't have to know about Plato and Aristotle to serve. You don't have to know Einstein's Theory of Relativity to serve. You don't have to know the second theory of thermodynamics in physics to serve. You only need a heart full of grace. A soul generated by love."

What I have learned and am still learning is that we have far too many people in the world with titles and very few people who are willing to pick up the towel to go to work and to serve others.

BONUS FROM JONAS
"Put up your titles, pick up your towels
and serve your way to greatness!"

BONUS FROM JONAS
"You don't have to be great to get started, but you
have to get started in order to be Great!"

Start right now. It is Now O'Clock!

I am reminded of when I was a teenager growing up in South Carolina. I was given the responsibility to go into the backyard, along with my brother, to dig a deep hole—at least 6 feet deep. We dug and dug, as deep as we could until we reached water. Then we took a pipe and drove the pipe as deep in the ground as we could. Then we took a second pipe and attached it to the first. We lubricated and sealed it to make sure there was no leak. Then, after that, we placed the final part to the pipe. That was called a pump.

Underneath the ground was a lot of cool, clear, sweet and refreshing water, virtually untapped. We wanted and needed the water for human consumption. However, in order for us to tap into the water, we had to first take some water out of a bucket and pour it into the pump to prime the pump. And we kept on pouring and kept on pumping...kept on pouring and kept on pumping. And, finally the water started coming out of the ground. At first, it was dirty, muddy, gray, not fit for drinking, but we kept on pumping. And after a while, the water became clearer and clearer. We were finally able to drink the clear, cool, clean, refreshing and sweet water, which quenched our thirst. We could also use it for cooking, bathing, and washing.

Someone may ask, "Jonas, what is your point?" Well, my point is that I know that there is greatness in each one of you, just lying dormant and ready to be tapped.

I am here to "prime your pump" to help you to realize your dreams, goals and aspirations, as well as to encourage you that although individuals will tell you that you can't make a positive difference that maybe you can make a dent. But I do not believe that.

I believe you can make a positive difference. All you have to do is to continue to prime your pump and keep on pumping. Prime and pump. Sometimes you are not going to achieve what you want right away...
Just keep on pumping. Sometimes people are going to talk about you... Keep on pumping. Sometimes people are going to lie about you... Keep on pumping. Sometimes family members are going to say to you, "No one in this family ever went to college." Just keep on pumping.

Sometimes you will feel discouraged... Keep on pumping.

You have been working on your dreams for a long time and it seems like nothing is happening. It doesn't seem like it is working. You want to give up. No. Keep on pumping.

Sometimes you feel like throwing in the towel, maybe you just lost your job and are feeling discouraged but keep on pumping. Maybe you are facing foreclosure on your home and I know it can be difficult. There are new options. Keep on pumping. Maybe your money is acting funny. Keep on pumping. Maybe you are having relationship issues. Don't give up. Just keep on pumping.

Don't ever stop until you make it to the top. Keep on pumping. The more you pump, the clearer the water becomes. The sweeter the water becomes...
Keep on pumping.

BONUS FROM JONAS
"When things go wrong, don't you go wrong with them."

The same reason I am sharing this true story with you is the same reason I am writing this book to you. I am stopping by in your mind just to let you know that in life you must prime your pump. Everything you need is in you already. Maybe it is lying dormant underneath all of the debris, all of the discouragement, and all of the past failures that have caused you to give up.

I challenge you to prime your pump again. You may feel tired, but keep on pumping. Things might not have turned out the way you want them to, but keep on pumping.
You might have been laid off from your job, but keep on pumping. Your husband or wife may have left you, and you are feeling so discouraged. Keep on pumping. Your children may be acting up, causing you sleepless nights...

BONUS FROM JONAS
"If you can't sleep at night don't stay awake counting sheep, turn and talk to the shepherd."

After that—keep on pumping.

You may even be having financial difficulties or other challenges. Whatever they are keep on pumping.

"Therefore, my beloved brethren, be ye steadfast, unmovable, always abounding in the work of the Lord, forasmuch as you know that your labor is not in vain in the Lord" (1st Corinthians 15:58).

In the end, if you do not give up, you will achieve whatever it is that you are pursuing. Whatever you are pursuing in life, it is also pursuing you. Again, having the mindset that I am going to achieve my dreams, or die in pursuit of them.

Booker T. Washington said, "You can't hold a man down without staying down with him." Do not let anything, or anybody hold you down or turn you around. Summon the *greatness* that is in you and wants to come out because...

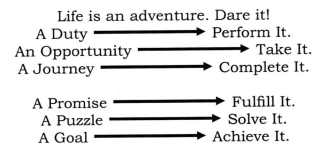

Life is an adventure. Dare it!
A Duty ⟶ Perform It.
An Opportunity ⟶ Take It.
A Journey ⟶ Complete It.

A Promise ⟶ Fulfill It.
A Puzzle ⟶ Solve It.
A Goal ⟶ Achieve It.

What is it that you want to achieve? Whatever you want to achieve, do not be afraid to ask for help. "Not because you are weak, but because you want to remain strong."

And I emphasize this bonus again:

BONUS FROM JONAS
"There's no defense against greatness. If there is a crack, then greatness will seep through. If there is no crack, then greatness will *break through!*"

As you pursue your greatness, you demonstrate it with a humble and selfless example. You also realize that it doesn't make any sense to beat a dead horse. The horse is dead so dismount and get a new horse.

When you are focusing on greatness you know that it is a full-time job and you do not have to shout it out, but show it out by your *conversation, conduct,* and your *character.* You spend your time building people up and not working to tear them down. "You know that big-minded people discuss ideas, average-minded people discuss events, but small-minded people discuss people because they fear their own potential."

Many times we allow our fear to paralyze and hold us back from realizing our greatness. I like what Zig Ziglar says about FEAR. In acrostics it is, "False Evidence Appearing Real." Often times we do not accomplish what we are designed to achieve because we believe that what we fear is real.

BONUS FROM JONAS
"If you face your fear, then you become fearless!"

I have learned that the subconscious mind can't distinguish between truth and error. If you tell yourself repeatedly that you cannot achieve something, your sub-conscience mind will remind you of all your past failures to make sure that you are right.

But if you develop the attitude that we spoke about earlier, an "I can do" attitude, then your sub-conscience mind would recall all of your successes, in essence to let you know that you are right and "You can do it!"

There are two things that paralyze people: The fear of success and the fear of failure. Since I have failed many times in the past, now I have learned the art of how to fail forward. Failure is an event, not a person. Instead of using the failure as a stumbling block use it as a stepping stone. Fear of failure stops many from even getting started. They get stuck in the stage of what I call, "paralysis of analysis." They allow fear to paralyze them. Eleanor Roosevelt once said, "No one can make you feel inferior without your consent." Don't give in to your frustrations, don't give in to your friends, don't give in to your foes, don't give in to your failures, don't give in to your finances...Don't give your consent to fear.

BONUS FROM JONAS
"People treat you the way that you train them!"

Fear of success equally retards progress toward your goals. Some people succeed and allow their success to cause them to believe that they are undeserving and not worthy of the success. Then, they sabotage themselves and return to a level of accomplishment that is more in harmony with what they believe they deserve. They are back in their comfort zone; satisfied with the life of mediocrity. Or are they? You are knocked down. Yes, but you are not knocked out! You can make a new choice. It's up to *you!* Get up from down there! Arise!

BONUS FROM JONAS
"You don't need a new revelation; what you need to do is obey the current information!"

You must have clear, specific, and calculated goals. I have said it before, but it bears repeating: It is amazing to me that most people have prepared for a two-week vacation every year but have not taken the time to design their lives.

BONUS FROM JONAS
"Sometimes people spend so much time
in planning their vacation that they never
fully realize their vocation."

Your vocation is your calling, why you are on this planet."
You must develop a plan for your journey to greatness!

BONUS FROM JONAS
"Instead of feeding your fear,
start fueling your future!"

In her book *Return to Love* Marianne Williamson wrote:
"Our deepest fear is not that we are inadequate.
Our deepest fear is that we are powerful beyond measure.
It is our light, not our darkness that most frightens us.
We ask ourselves, who am I to be brilliant, gorgeous,
talented and fabulous? Actually, who are you not to be?
You are a child of God.
Your playing small doesn't serve the world.
There is nothing enlightened about shrinking so that other
people won't feel insecure around you.
We were born to make manifest the glory of God within us.
It is not just in some of us; it's in everyone.
And, as we let our own light shine, we unconsciously give
other people permission to do the same.
As we are liberated from our own fear,
our presence automatically liberates others."

This book *How To Fly Like An Eagle With Wings Like A
Wimp!* is about liberation to set you and your greatness free.
You were born a winner.

I'd like to take you back on a brief journey to prove that
you are a winner. Now, I need your help. Do you remember
when you were fifteen years old? Hold up your hand. Okay,
what about when you were ten years old? Hands, please.
All right, what about when you were five years old? Hands,
please. Now, let us go all the way back to the time of your

conception, when you were just a sperm.

Up to 500 million sperm were released at the same time that you were released. You out-swam 500 million sperm in order to get here. You are a winner.

Now, you say, "Oh, Jonas, I can't even swim." Yes, I know.

But you swam once. Uphill. It was only one egg coming down that long, dark tunnel and you got there first. You will never face those kinds of odds the rest of your life. You were born a winner. In fact, give yourself a round of applause for being a winner. If you want, from this point on to continue to be a winner, you must *win* (Work It Now).

You are now moving to a new level, not only realizing your own potential, but helping others realize theirs.

I like what Jackie Robinson said, "A life is not important except in the impact it has on other lives." If you want to be a Sir Edmond, and climb your Mt. Everest, to get to the top, you must first get off of the bottom. You cannot go up, without first getting up.

BONUS FROM JONAS
"In order to go up you must first get up. In order to get up you must first look up. Look up and live!"

Oliver Wendell Holmes said, "Greatness is not in where we stand, but in what direction we are moving. We must sail sometimes with the wind and sometimes against it. But sail we must, and not drift, nor lie at anchor."

Now, I'm going to talk to you about manifesting your greatness. It is like a woman who is pregnant and ready to deliver her baby. You have been carrying your dream around from its conception. You were nurturing it, you have been feeding it. You even woke up sometimes with morning sickness.

Now it is time to deliver your baby. Your dream!

Before you can deliver a natural child you will go through stages of labor pains. At the early stage of labor the pain is mild and inconsistent. However, as you progress through labor the pain becomes more intense and regular. The baby is ready to be born. Just before the baby is born, the labor pain is at the greatest intensity. Only *pushing*, despite the excruciating pain, will bring forth the new child.

Whether you are a man or a woman, you are pregnant with your dreams and now ready to give birth. It is *your* time to push. You must be willing to push past negativity. *Push* past it like you have never done before. Push past your fears. Push past old beliefs. Past your old self of complacency and mediocrity. Push past your educational background on toward manifesting your greatness! You must push past low self-esteem. Now that you have a larger vision of yourself, you push continuously because you understand the process of giving birth to your new baby. Your dream!

Using the birth analogy, when you begin to push, it seems as though the baby will never come. However, as you continue to push you can see the head come out. When you see the head that gives you more motivation to keep on pushing. After a while, you see the shoulders; suddenly, the torso the buttocks, and legs, and eventually the entire baby appears.

BONUS FROM JONAS
"People do not care about your labor pains in life, all they want you to do is to show them the baby!"

Accomplishing your dreams is no different. As you continue to push past the challenges you will begin to see the small manifestations of your vision. And as you continue pushing you will see more and more positive results, which gives you more and more motivation to keep on pushing.

What is PUSH?

Push

Until

Something Positive

Happens

Making calls, making contacts, communicating to other people on a daily basis what your dreams are, what you have to offer and how that can benefit them.

Be willing to take that class, talk to a coach, read inspirational and motivational books, which will lead you to tap into your positive thoughts and follow through with positive action.

Psychologists indicate that each one of us has about 50,000 thoughts per day.

If we would only be proactive with just one or two positive thoughts, then we would be able to achieve the level of greatness that is within us. Someone once said,

"I would rather take risks to learn to fly, than to live a safe predictable life where crawling would be my greatest accomplishment."

Now that you have made up your mind that crawling days are over and flying days are here. *Congratulations!* Now is the time to allow that greatness "to bud, to bloom and to blossom" into a bright and beautiful future.

It was Carl Mayes who said, "Those who can see the invisible can do the impossible."

BONUS FROM JONAS
**"Now, you have realized that all there is to it.
Is to do it."**

Because...

BONUS FROM JONAS
**"The only place that you will find success
before work is in the dictionary."**

Celebrate your victory! Now that you have succeeded, make sure to celebrate. Create *joy* in the Journey. Build in celebration as you go and grow.

BONUS FROM JONAS
**"Don't make the celebration a destination, but make it
the documentation for your success!"**

Keep all of your data to document this manifestation of truth, because...

BONUS FROM JONAS
"Success leaves clues!"

The next thing that I want to emphasize in pursuing your greatness is not only bringing your dreams to reality, but helping others to accomplish theirs' as well.

If you want to make a difference for one year. Plant grain. If you want to make a difference for ten years plant trees. But if you want to make a difference for one hundred years, grow people.

BONUS FROM JONAS
"The greatness of a man is not in the number of his servants, but in the number of people he serves."

When you "Go For Greatness," you want to take as many people with you as you can. Because we are interdependent beings: I need you and you need me.

Dr. Martin Luther King, Jr. once said, "If I can help somebody, as I pass along. If I can cheer somebody with a word or a song, if I can show somebody he's traveling wrong, then my living would not be in vain." This is why I wrote this book, *How To Fly Like An Eagle With Wings Like A Wimp!*

If I can just help somebody to live their purpose with a passion then my living would not have been in vain.

As you achieve Great Success make sure to develop Successors. Help others to succeed. What kind of legacy are you working to leave behind? Again, I want to ask you, "Are you making a dent, or are you making a positive difference?" Now, that you have achieved your greatness, I encourage and challenge you to reach back to move from success to significance...

HELP SOMEBODY!

BONUS FROM JONAS
"The list below is not designed to depress you, but it is designed to bless you!
Help Somebody and Help Yourself!"

HELP SOMEBODY!

1. In 1999, 3,000 people were being laid off every day in America. In 2008, 3 million jobs were lost. In 2009, 6 million people were unemployed. In the first quarter of 2010, 7 million people are out of work and the unemployment rate nationally is 9.7 percent, down from 10 percent in December 2009. The August 2010 Bureau of Labor Statistics Report lists the number of Americans out of work at 14.9 million.

2. The National Foreclosure Ticker shows foreclosures in the United States as of January 1, 2010, at over 2 million. 6,600 new foreclosures a day; one every 13 seconds.

3. There are 46 million Americans who have no health insurance. On March 23, 2010, President Barack Obama signed into law the Patient Protection and Affordable Care Act which makes health insurance more affordable; reducing premium costs for tens of millions of families and small business owners who are priced out of coverage. It helps 32 million Americans afford health care who do not get it today. Under this plan, 95 percent of Americans will be insured.

4. In 2008, 65 percent of all revenue generated in the US came from Small Business. Small Businesses create most of the nation's new jobs, employ about half of the nation's private sector work force, and provide half of the nation's non-farm, private, real GDP (gross domestic product) as well as a significant share of innovations. In 2008, there were 29.6 million small businesses; 6 million employer firms and 23 million nonemployer firms.

5. Forty to forty-four million American adults or 20 to 21 percent of the people in America can't read.

6. Forty million Americans live in poverty; 13 million or 18 percent are children under 18 years old. One of every 8 children under age 12 in the United States goes to bed hungry every night.

HELP SOMEBODY!

7. Forty-five million children worldwide are starving. Every year 15 million children die of hunger. Every day almost 16,000 children die of hunger. One child every 5 seconds—worldwide.
8. One third of American adults are obese or 64 million Americans and 17 percent of the population are children who are obese.
9. One million teen-aged girls become pregnant each year. In 2006, 435,436 births were to girls aged 15 to 19 years old. In some communities teenage pregnancy is no longer the exception but the rule.
10. Self-esteem is at an all-time low.
11. Drug abuse is at an all-time high. In 2007, it was estimated that 22 million Americans (9 percent of the population) aged 12 years or older were substance abusers.
12. In 2006, suicide was the 11th leading cause of death in the United States.
13. Nationwide 7,000 students per day drop out of school and 1 million drop out of high school each year. 1,500 teenagers drop out of school every day. One per minute.
14. In 2006, guns killed 3,218 teens and children. 135,000 youth bring guns to school every day. 30 get wounded every day. 10 die every day.
15. 2,300 Americans die daily of cancer. By 2010 cancer will be the leading cause of death in the United States. In 2008 there were 1 million new cases of cancer in the US and 565,650 Americans died of cancer in 2008.
16. There are 7 million Americans in prison: 1 in every 31 adults. Black males have the highest rate of imprisonment at 7 times higher than that of white males and 3 times higher than that of Hispanic males. In 2006, there were 3,042 Black males in prison for every 100,000 Black males in the United States at large. In 2003, 10 percent of the Black male population (aged 25 to 29) was in prison; 2 percent of Hispanic males; and 1 percent of white males.

HELP SOMEBODY!

17. On September 11, 2001, America experienced a horrific attack on New York City's World Trade Center, the Pentagon in Washington, DC, and the aborted attack in Pennsylvania. Approximately 3,000 innocent Americans died; leaving thousands more loved ones behind.
18. Since 2001 America has been in wars against Iraq and Afghanistan. In these two raging wars, it was reported that 5,356 American soldiers have lost their lives and thousands others have been injured.
19. American families are still reeling from the Fort Hood, Texas Massacre on Thursday November 7, 2009. Done at the hands of an American soldier, 12 soldiers and 1 civilian were killed; 38 people were wounded.
20. As a result of the January 12, 2010, earthquake that occurred in Haiti, 210,000 people have died. Haiti is a country with 9 million people; one-third of them live in Port-Au-Prince, the capital.

With all of the various areas I have stated in this chapter, there is something positive all of us can do to help somebody.

Even if you are faced with some difficult challenges yourself, and others are working diligently to influence you not to do anything to help anybody, I am encouraging you to do it anyway.

I will leave you with these 10 challenges entitled, "Anyway," by Howard Ferguson.

1. People are illogical, unreasonable, and self-centered.
   LOVE THEM ANYWAY.
2. If you do good people will accuse you of selfish, ulterior motives.
   DO GOOD ANYWAY.
3. If you are successful, you will win false friends and true enemies.
   SUCCEED ANYWAY.
4. The good you do today will be forgotten tomorrow.
   DO GOOD ANYWAY.
5. Honesty and frankness make you vulnerable.
   BE HONEST AND FRANK ANYWAY.

6. The biggest men with the biggest ideas can be shot down by the smallest men with the smallest minds.
THINK BIG ANYWAY.
7. People favor underdogs, but follow only top dogs.
FIGHT FOR A FEW UNDERDOGS ANYWAY.
8. What you spend years building may be destroyed overnight.
BUILD ANYWAY.
9. People really need help but may attack you if you do help them.
HELP THEM ANYWAY.
10. Give the world the best you have and you'll get kicked in the teeth.
GIVE THE WORLD THE BEST YOU HAVE ANYWAY.

As I bring this chapter to a close, you have given birth to your dreams. You have pushed until something positive has happened. You have decided that you are going to leave a positive legacy for those you love and for others to follow. You have answered the call emphatically and you went out and helped somebody...And you did it anyway.

You realized...

BONUS FROM JONAS
"That people really do not need a hand out, but they need a hand up."

Congratulations to you! However, I want you to realize that now you are at *one* level of greatness! You must continue to do all of the right things to maintain and grow to higher heights; then you will move from success to significance. Everyone is not going to give you encouraging words, accolades, praise, or recognition. You must know why you are doing what you are doing. If you do not know why you are doing what you are doing then you won't do it for long.

BONUS FROM JONAS
"A huddle a day keeps mediocrity away and it welcomes greatness in to stay! *Welcome in, Greatness!*"

"Since Greatness Is Possible, Excellence Is Not Enough! Go for Greatness!"

Chapter Five

Laughter

L-Laughter

In this chapter we are going to talk about the value and importance of laughter in your life on a daily basis. I am not talking about demeaning or degrading other people. And certainly, I am not talking about dirty, obscene, or vulgar kinds of laughter. I am advocating clean and wholesome laughter that will enrich your life and the lives of those whom you love.

In essence, doing what you love to do. I read a book entitled, *Do What You Love and the Money Will Follow*. To paraphrase:

BONUS FROM JONAS
"Do what you love and the joy will follow."

Proverbs 17:22 says, "A merry heart doeth good like a medicine: But a broken spirit drieth the bones." Statistics indicate and reveal amazing evidence that emphasizes the importance of laughter. It has significant health benefits, spiritually, physically, emotionally, psychologically, and relationally.

Consider this description of laughter. The neural circuits in your brain begin to reverberate. Chemical and electrical impulses start flowing rapidly through your body.

A special gland releases certain chemicals in your body,

which race through your blood. Your body temperature rises half a degree, your pulse rate and blood pressure increases, your arteries and thoracic muscles contract, your vocal cords quiver, and your face contorts. Pressure builds in your lungs. Your lower jaw suddenly drops uncontrollably and breath bursts from your mouth at nearly 70 miles an hour.

This is a clinical description of laughter.

At Northwestern University, a study conducted under strict scientific conditions, revealed that the act of laughing massages the heart, stimulates the blood circulation, and helps the lungs breath easier. Laughter is considered "internal jogging."

Another test at Fordham University reinforced the conclusion that, "Laughter benefits the heart, lungs, stomach and other organs. It relaxes our tensions and promotes a feeling of well being."

One of the things that stuck out in my mind as I read the study on laughter is that the average adult only laughs about 15 times per day. Preschoolers laugh 450 times per day. Why is this? Adults experience and deal with life challenges constantly and sometimes in maladjusted ways. I have learned and am still learning that often times we take ourselves too seriously. I believe we should take life seriously, but take ourselves lightly and laugh.

There are at least seven health-related benefits of laughter.

1. It massages your heart.
2. It lowers your blood pressure.
3. It releases stress.
4. It prolongs your life.
5. It helps stimulate your digestive system.
6. It improves your blood circulation.
7. It reduces tension.

Anything that does this much for our health we definitely should do more of it.

"Hearty laughter is a good way to jog internally without having to go outdoors." (11)

Dr. Norman Cousins wrote a book entitled the *Anatomy of an Illness*, which told about a debilitating illness he overcame with laughter. He watched funny movies and stories.

I love laughing. I love watching funny, hilarious, and clean movies.

I love clean jokes and funny stories. In fact, I seek out reasons and environments that are conducive to healthy laughter. I have even learned a very tough lesson and that is…"be able to laugh at yourself."

"…Weeping may endure for a night, but joy cometh in the morning" (Psalms 30:5). The reason why angels can fly is because they take themselves lightly.

I remember that some of the most difficult times in my life were between 1990 and 2000; I lost my oldest sister Lillian in 1990; my brother Joseph in 1993, and then I lost my baby brother Abraham in 2000. We also lost several other members of the family. It was an unhappy, painful and sad time for the Gadson family.

I remember a true story from Abraham's funeral in the year 2000. Abraham and I grew up together and we had a close relationship. So when he all of a sudden, at the age of 45, took ill and died, it was devastating to me, as well as to the family. This was even more difficult because between the years 1990 and 2000, we lost eleven family members to death.

When I got the call that Lillian had passed away, I had to go. Oh, that was so hurtful, the day that we buried our oldest sister. Even more hurtful was the moment we got back to the house from my oldest sister's funeral when my brother, Joseph had a stroke and remained ill until he died in 1993.

In the meantime, my uncle and my aunt, and more relatives passed away, and I went back and forth Down South hurting, crying, pleading, and praying. "I know some of you have lost someone that you have loved and you miss them. It's alright to cry, it's all right to pray, it's alright to get yourself some counseling." When I traveled home for the last funeral in 2000, my baby brother Abraham had died and I was simply out of words. The motivator, "Mr. Enthusiastic," had nothing to say. It's unlike me to be out of words, since I love talking to people. I want to reiterate what I stated before: I've never met a group of people that I didn't love talking to. Every group brings me joy. Now I admit, some people bring me joy when they enter the room, but others bring me joy when they leave the room. Nevertheless, they all bring me joy.

When I arrived home to my mother's house, I thought, "What am I going to say to her? She's lost another child." When I got to the house and opened the door, my mother solved that challenge for me. She ran to me and threw her arms around me and she said, "Son, I've been through the mill, but I refuse to grind." We are going to go through challenges. We are going to go through tough times, but don't ever give up. We were traveling back from the graveyard after the burial of my brother Abraham, and everybody was silent and hurting. Everyone felt really down and out, especially me. I was not only upset because of the loss of my brother, but I was drained from traveling so much.

Some moments passed while driving back in the limousine, and suddenly, my oldest brother from Brooklyn, New York, Joe Louis, said, "You know the way the Gadsons are dying, by the time I die, there may not be any place for you all to bury me."

I replied, "Brother, if you are that concerned about having some place for you to be buried, you can take my place."

We loosened up. We laughed through our tears. What I learned from that experience is that even in the loss of my brother, when we were experiencing pain and sorrow; we were still able to find a moment for laughter. I concluded that we could find laughter even in the toughest times. Humor is at times essential to bring us out of the deepest times of despair. Regardless of your circumstances, challenges or adversities, it is okay to take life seriously, but don't take yourself so seriously because life is short, and you can't get out of life alive.

There was a study done many years ago to emphasize the danger and the damage that you can do to your health when you keep things inside of you. Some scientists did a test in the laboratory using individuals who were hurting, grieving, who had lost loved ones, or had unresolved issues that had been eating away at them. And as the individuals were crying from the depths of their souls, they took the tears and put them in a test tube. They discovered that those tears were toxic: So powerful, that if you weren't careful, if you drank them, you could die instantaneously.

Then they did the same experiment with another group of individuals that were happy, jubilant, and healthy, and they were laughing from the depths of their souls. And they took their tears and put them in a test tube as well. What they discovered was that if you were to drink those tears, they were sweet, palatable, and digestible.

The point that I am working to bring home is that laughter has so many health benefits, that all of us can stand a dose of healthy, happy laughter. "There is a time to cry and there is a time to laugh" (Ecclesiastes 3:4). The challenge is to know which one to do when.

We need to know what time it is.

When was the last time that you had a down-home, belly hurting, eyes-rolled-up with tears, and were out-of-control and overtaken in a positive way with laughter? You might say, "I don't know." Is that your final answer? Well, it is time to laugh again. I am talking about that inner joy, the kind that is not predicated upon external events.

What I have learned is that it is not what is going on around you that takes away that inner joy, but rather, what is going on inside of you. Allow me to make another brief distinction between happiness and joy. Happiness is because of...and joy is in spite of.... It is a choice.

Joy is an inside feeling manifested by a positive outside explosion through laughter. I know that things might be bad right now, but I have joy in knowing that there is a brighter day ahead. There is a song that most of us have heard. The title is "One Day at a Time." It is great for those who are at the point in their lives when they can enjoy their accomplishments one day at a time. The family is healthy and their jobs are secure. They have money in all of their pockets. They live in a beautiful home with two cars in the garage. They take a five-week vacation every year at their summer cottage.

They have stocks and bonds, mutual funds and a 401K retirement plan. So one day at a time is great. They love it.

However, for anyone who is going through tough times, one day at a time is too much. Very few people are living in this place. I have created a new version of the song, which I call "One Second at a Time." I encourage people dealing with tough times to adopt the version of the song, "One Second at a Time."

Then that one second turns into two seconds and pretty soon you have an hour. And before you know it, you have accomplished a day. With the right kind of support and tools, eventually they will make it to "one day at a time."

BONUS FROM JONAS
"What looks like the end of the road is really a bend in the road."

That is why it is so important that you find out for yourself what your purpose is and live it with a passion. And stay true to your value.

BONUS FROM JONAS
"Because when your value is clear, your decision is easy!"

As I close this chapter on laughter, I want to leave you with what Ralph Waldo Emerson said:

"To laugh often and much: to win the respect of intelligent people and the affection of children: to earn the appreciation of honest critics, and endure the betrayal of false friends: to appreciate beauty, to find the best in others: to leave the world a bit better, whether by a healthy child, a garden patch, or a redeemed social condition: to know even one life has breathed easier because you have lived. This is to have succeeded!"

Chapter Six

Extra Mile

E-Extra Mile

CONGRATULATIONS! YOU HAVE JUST LANDED on the road that's called, "the Extra Mile."

BONUS FROM JONAS
"I got the general area scan let me zoom
in to see where I'm going to land!"

BONUS FROM JONAS
"On the road that is labeled, "Extra Mile,"
You never have to concern yourself about a traffic jam!
Because it is the road less traveled!"

The road less traveled is for eagles because an eagle is a solitary bird. As the scripture says, "The road that leads to life is straight and narrow and few there be that find it" (Matthew 7:13-14). Let's get up, get on, and get going!

I remember vividly on Saturday October 28, 2008, as I prepared to go to vote for the next president of the United States of America. On that day, it wasn't too cold and it wasn't too hot. The sun was shining brightly. It was the right moment. I am thankful for this day. What made it exceptional wasn't necessarily the condition of the weather, it was the winning attitude of the people who were in line preparing to vote.

The voting line was over a mile long with people of all colors and backgrounds in it. When I first arrived, a few people mentioned, "Oh, I'll come back later; the line is so long," But I persuaded them to stay. I stood in line for four and a half hours as I waited to vote. And the line continued to grow even longer as the day wore on. Everyone was interacting like a community. People held each other's place in line when the elderly got tired to encourage them to go to their cars and sit for a while. It was a supportive and caring environment. There was no bickering, no complaining, no profanity, no pushing, no drunkenness. No disrespectful behavior. Even though it was hours, it was hours of moments. So many stood in line. Standing. And they didn't say a word. They stood!

They demonstrated a picture of quiet strength and power. I was so encouraged by the positive behavior that was demonstrated and the peace that followed because of it. Even the children who were with their parents behaved exceptionally.

This reminded me of the old African proverb, which says, "It takes a village to raise a child." It was a picture-perfect moment. And I was inside of the frame. I was able to come out of the picture frame and snap the picture. It was a life transformational moment. A time to reflect, to meditate, and I captured it.

BONUS FROM JONAS
"It is very difficult to take the picture when you are inside of the picture frame!"

I stood in line for four and a half hours in the Deep South—in beautiful Beaufort, South Carolina—outside! And I learned in life that you can do whatever you decide to do! I was not standing alone. I had just lost my mother; I was standing for her. I stood for my brothers and my sister who had died and didn't get to see this day. I stood for my ancestors. I stood for so many other Americans like women, Native Americans, and others who were denied the right to vote. It was exhilarating to be a part of this historical moment. I was standing with so many other Americans. And it created so many precious memories...and when I was finished I wasn't tired. I stood there because I wanted my vote to count.

BONUS FROM JONAS
"If you don't vote, you don't have a voice!"

Who do you think that each candidate voted for? Yes. You are right. They voted for themselves. Sometimes in life, the reason that you are not winning is that you refuse to vote for yourself.

A lot of times we will vote for others and help them to win, but we refuse to vote for ourselves and then wonder why we lose. Who are you voting for? You should be willing to vote for yourself first.

BONUS FROM JONAS
"You've got to be in it in order to win it!"

In voting for yourself, sometimes you must be willing to stand in a long line.

BONUS FROM JONAS
"If you know what you are standing for, you'll be given what you need to stand on! But if you don't know what you are standing for, you won't stand at all or you won't stand for long!"

I remember election night—Tuesday, November 4, 2008—when history was made. America, along with the world was watching, waiting to see who was going to be the next president of the United States. Many of us were watching as I was, sitting on the edge of our seats at home, glued to the television, waiting for the results to come in. Then we found out: The 44th President of the United States of America was voted into office. Senator Barack Obama won the election. *Wow!* He was the first African-American man to become President of the United States of America! This is the highest office in the land; the leader of the most powerful country in the world. It is an enormous task to capture such a world-shaking event and restrict it to a couple of paragraphs.

There was joy! Excitement! Tears of happiness! Exclamations of disbelief! Jubilee and rejoicing! And many other overwhelming emotions! Then in Chicago, the new President Obama, his wife, and his little girls, and the new

Vice President Joe Biden, his wife, and his family were on stage as newly elected President Obama gave his acceptance speech. Americans had a new vision of what was possible! Newly elected President Obama started off his speech: "If there is anyone out there who still doubts that America is a place where all things are possible; who still wonders if the dream of our founders is alive in our time; who still questions the power of our democracy, tonight is your answer..." (12)

It was a tremendous experience for me to witness on January 20, 2009, the first African-American man to be inaugurated into the office of the 44th President of the United States of America. President Barack Obama! Millions of Americans obtained tickets to the Inauguration. This was the largest crowd ever in the history of America to be a part of the Presidential Inaugural Ceremonies in Washington, DC. President Obama had opened these ceremonies up to every American citizen. We all had an invitation to come. Whoever could be there. And millions more of Americans wanted to be in Washington, DC, but like me couldn't be.

Although I wasn't in Washington, DC, physically, I was very much present by watching it on television; it was like being there from start to finish. It is estimated that millions of Americans attended the Inaugural Ceremonies for President Barack Obama. The attendance was so high that there were thousands of Americans with tickets who were turned away.

The Inauguration of President Barack Obama represented a new era. We as Americans, 310 million strong, had the privilege and the pleasure to participate in bringing in a new era for America and for the world. (13)

All Americans have benefited from the right to vote in a democracy. A right that many have fought for and lived and died for. We are blessed to be a part of the greatest country in the world: America. Personally, in all of my years of living, I have never seen or heard of a group of people leaving various countries, leaving including America saying, "If I can only get to China...Germany...Korea...Russia." They have been dying to get to America. Their mindset was "If I can only make it to America..." And sometimes we take the blessings that were given to us for granted.

On January 12, 2010, Haiti was rocked with an earthquake registering 7.0 on the Richter scale. More than 210,000 people lost their lives. It is estimated that 20,000 people had been dying daily. People from all over the world were trying to help save the Haitian people. In the midst of this, the Haitians were doing everything with a limited amount of resources to save themselves. This didn't stop them from doing what they could, versus focusing on what they couldn't. If they had stopped their persistence—their resilience—and the care that they demonstrated toward their fellow man, there would have been more dead.

A lot of people were saved because of the persistence of the Haitian people who did not have any equipment but they had a mind to want to help. Then they had a heart of compassion. They were compelled. And then they reached down with their hands and went to work. They got involved. They were not focused on what they couldn't do. They were focused on what they could do and they did it. There was a young girl who was trapped and covered by concrete. They finally got to her and her leg was broken.

She said that she expected to be delivered; rescued. And she was. She had a mind of expectancy. She didn't even consider that she was going to die. And she didn't.

There was a 15-year-old girl who was buried and covered by the concrete. It was reported that when the building collapsed, she was near the bathroom and had access to some water. They said this attributed to her survival for 15 days. When they did get to her and got her out, she was extremely dehydrated. She was one of the people who was covered the longest. She held on and they got to her in time. And she survived!

These two incidents are examples of "the best of humanity," and there were literally hundreds of true stories like these that were happening daily in Haiti.

Now that's the resilience of the human spirit and the power of God. This is what happens when people reach out, reach down, and reach up. The Haitians didn't have time to focus on what they had lost. If they had let that consume them, the casualties would have been greater and they could have been one of them. They took the time to focus on what was left. What you see is what you are looking for.

If you focus on the positive you can help more people. "Don't focus on what you have lost; focus on what you have left."

This is a long-term recovery. However, in the midst of disaster, there are stories demonstrating the best of humanity.

And you are seeing the outpouring of support of money, food, medicine, people leaving from America going to a torn, destroyed area to help others. That is the *best* of humanity. That is what I am all about.

BONUS FROM JONAS
"Even in the worst of circumstances you can demonstrate the *best* of humanity!"

We are praying for Haiti daily and let all of us express our love through giving. I have learned that

BONUS FROM JONAS
"I'm being blessed for the express purpose of being a blessing!"

I will continue to give. Not to give to get. The scripture says in Acts 20:35, "...It is more blessed to give than to receive."

What are you doing that is positive, not only to help the people in Haiti?

What about the people right in your country? In your community? When you die what kind of legacy are you leaving? What kind of lessons are you teaching?

I have learned...

BONUS FROM JONAS
"That the best lesson is better caught than taught!"
When you die, what kind of legacy are you going to leave?

I am reminded of the true story that was told about Dr. Alfred Nobel. He woke up one morning and read in the newspaper his premature obituary. And it said "the merchant of death is dead. Dr. Alfred Nobel who became rich by finding ways of killing more people faster than ever before, died yesterday." They had made a mistake.

But he had an epiphany. He realized that he didn't want to be remembered as a killer and that motivated him to get busy. He created the Nobel Peace Prize. So that when he died, he was known as the "Merchant of Peace." Now, when we hear of Alfred Nobel, we don't think of killing, dynamite, or bombs, because the prize is awarded to the person who strives to bring about peace.

How do you want to be remembered? If you are living, you still have time to transform that legacy. You can start to write a new one right now. Just as you are reading this book. You can say no to negativity and destructive living and say yes to positivity and productive living.

Now he has left a legacy so that when people think of the Nobel Peace Prize they think of peace and not destruction. He worked diligently to change the negative things that were associated with him. Before he was being rewarded and remembered for killing. After he changed his behavior, habits and lifestyle, he was remembered as a person who represented peace. If you are being remembered in a negative way now, you too can change your legacy. You have to take the initiative.

BONUS FROM JONAS
"You are the change that you are looking for!"

You can't see the best in others when you refuse to see the best in *you*."

In this book, we have already explored in detail the knowledge, the skills, the mental toughness, the discipline and the tenacity that it will take to achieve your dreams, your goals, and your aspirations. You've been given the tools that you can use.

BONUS FROM JONAS
"Education is part of the equation, but execution is the solution!"

I will show you how "teamwork makes the dream work" and that "together everyone achieves *more*." As you continue on this road that is called the Extra Mile, I will teach you how to fly longer, faster, achieve more than *ever* before and take your loved ones with you—How to Fly in a Victory Formation.

When you see geese flying around in a "V" formation, you might be interested in knowing what facts scientists have discovered about why they fly that way.

Fact 1: As each bird flaps its wings, it creates an updraft for the bird immediately following. By flying in a "V" formation, the whole flock adds at least 71 percent greater flying range than each bird flew on its own.

True: People who share a common direction and sense of community can get where they are going quicker, and easier because they are traveling on the trust of one another.

Fact 2: Whenever a goose falls out of formation, it suddenly feels the drag and resistance of trying to go it alone. And it quickly gets back into formation to take advantage of the lifting power of the bird immediately in front.

True: There is strength and safety in numbers when traveling in the same direction with those with whom we share a common goal.

Fact 3: When the lead goose gets tired, he rotates back into the wing and another goose flies point.

True: It pays to take turns doing hard jobs.

Fact 4: The geese honk from behind to encourage those up front to keep up their speed.

True: We all need to be remembered with active support and praise.

Fact 5: When a goose gets sick or is wounded and falls out, two geese fall out of formation and follow him down to help and protect him. They stay with him until the crisis resolves. And then they launch out on their own, or with another formation to catch up with the group.

True: "We must stand by each other in times of need."—Author Unknown

BONUS FROM JONAS
"A true friend walks in when everyone else walks out."

I am your friend and I am here to help you that together we can fly and gain our victory. And sometimes in life on the road less traveled, you are going to have some obstacles. What you have learned in this book will help you to deal with your obstacles.

Obstacles are not designed to stop you; they are designed to start you, to strengthen you and to prevent you from sinking. You too, can be like the tea kettle.

BONUS FROM JONAS
"When the tea kettle is up to its neck in hot water. It sings."

As I help you to build a reservoir with new knowledge, new skills, and new techniques then I want you to connect to your reservoir a river that will flow from heart to heart, and from life to life to make a positive impact on your faith, on your family and on your friends. Now you can make a greater impact in your community, in the country and ultimately in the world. But it is not going to happen overnight. It will require, as I indicated earlier in the book, a lot of hard work. And *you* are worth it.

A bamboo tree takes five years for it to grow to its full potential. That means it requires on our part, a lot of patience, persistence, and perseverance. It requires of us...

BONUS FROM JONAS
"To never give up, to never give in, and to never give out because it is always too early to quit! Because a winner never quits and a quitter never wins!"

The first year in planting the bamboo tree you have to water it and nurture it every single day. Can you imagine for a moment, watering one spot where you plant the bamboo tree for 365 days in a row? If you miss one day, you lose the bamboo tree.

The second year, you must do the same thing. The third year, the same thing. Now at this time your family, friends, and your faith are tested like never before. Can you imagine people coming to you, asking you the question. "What are you doing? I've been noticing you for the last three years. Watering and nurturing the same spot. And nothing is growing. Are you sure that you are alright?" And you say, "Yes. I am fine. I am growing a bamboo tree." They reply, "I don't see anything. Even Stevie Wonder or David Paterson can see that there's nothing happening. Why don't you give up?"

But you don't. The fourth year, you follow the same process every single day. But in the fifth year, around about the sixth week, your bamboo tree shoots out of the ground and it grows ninety feet. Now the question is, "Did this tree grow instantaneously or did it take almost five years?" And sometimes going the extra mile is going to take all of your time, talent, and your treasures to make your dreams come to reality.

What a lot of people don't realize in the bamboo tree analogy is that the moment you plant it, it starts growing. But it grows down deep first. Because the tree is top heavy. It must grow 90 feet down before it can grow 90 feet up. When it grows up, it has its roots planted by the rivers of water that it shall not be moved.

BONUS FROM JONAS
"Part of going the extra mile is making sure that your roots are planted in absolutes!"

It was wisely said that in order to grow grain it takes one year; to grow trees it takes ten years, but to grow people it takes 100 years. I believe in growing people. Now, I am keenly aware that we are living in a microwave, quick-fix society. We want everything right now. We want instant oatmeal, we want instant coffee, we want instant weight loss, and we want instant success.

As I indicated before, the only place where you will find success before work is in the dictionary. There are times that we must crockpot our dreams, our goals, and our aspirations; to allow them to marinate and simmer in the juice that is going to fuel our future. I encourage you to keep on "keeping on."

BONUS FROM JONAS
"When things go wrong, don't you go wrong with them!"

Don't Quit

When things go wrong as they sometimes will,
When the road you are trudging seems all uphill,
When the funds are low and the debts are high,
And you want to smile but you have to sigh,
When care is pressing you down a bit.
Rest if you must, but don't quit.
Life is queer with its twists and turns,
As every one of us sometimes learns,
And many a person turns about
When they might have won had they stuck it out.
Don't give up though the pace seems slow.
You may succeed with another blow.
Often the struggler has given up
When he might have captured the victor's cup;
And he learned too late when the night came down,
How close he was to the golden crown.
Success is failure turned inside out.
So stick to the fight when you are hardest hit,
It is when things seem the worst that you must not quit."
—Unknown

It is important that we remain teachable.

BONUS FROM JONAS
"We can always better our best!"

Sometimes we can be our own worst enemy by not being willing to alter our course.

BONUS FROM JONAS
"Sometimes God calms the sea,
and other times God calms me!"

The story has been told of a young naval officer who was given his first assignment at sea. He was determined that nobody would push him around or disrespect his authority. One stormy night he saw a bright light coming toward his ship, so he sent a message ahead: "Alter your course by ten degrees south." Immediately, a message came back to him, "Alter your course by ten degrees north."

The young officer was infuriated. Such disrespect for authority. Such defiance. So he sent a second message, "Alter
your course by ten degrees south...*this is the Captain.*" Then
the message came back..."Alter *your* course by ten degrees
north...*this is the Lighthouse. Your choice.*" This book has
been written to help you to alter your course. It serves as
your lighthouse that will shine and illuminate your path so
you can see your future clearly.

This book is designed to educate, inspire, and motivate
you to greatness!

Harriet Tubman was a great example of how we can go
the extra mile to help our fellow man today. Harriet Tubman
was born free, not a slave. She was born into a slave condition, but yearned in her heart to be free as God intended all
of us to be.

She fought for years and years for her freedom, after hard
work, after persisting and after being caught and beaten,
bruised and battered over and over again she sustained a
head injury that plagued her for the rest of her life. But she
didn't let that stop her from leading former slaves to freedom
on what is now called the Underground Railroad.

She had a mission statement: "Freedom or death." She
had the mindset and the tenacity that said, "Either I am going
to achieve my freedom, or I am going to die in the process of
pursuing it." In pursuing your dreams, goals and aspirations,
you have to have that same mindset. Either I am going to
achieve it, or I am going to die in the process of pursuing it.

With this commitment and dedication, Harriet Tubman
achieved her mission and came to be known as the Black
"Moses." She finally reached freedom when she made it to
Canada. However, she was not content with this newfound
freedom, knowing that her mother, father, siblings, and other
people were still in bondage. Now Harriet Tubman could have
said, "Let everybody else fend for themselves. Let everyone
else pull themselves up by their own boot straps." Today,
many people whom we are mentoring have neither boots nor
straps, yet they need help from us to pull them up.

The only time that we should look down upon another
human being is when we are looking down to help them
up. Contrary to popular belief, there is only one race, and
that race is the human race, and we all are a part of it.

When Ms. Harriet Tubman made it to the North, she thought, "There are others back there who are suffering and being beaten and abused."

She wasn't able to enjoy her freedom when she knew so many other people were hurting. I challenge you as you finish reading this book to "go back" and help somebody.

Now, Harriet Tubman didn't go back only one time, or two times, or even three times. She went back *nineteen* more times. Sometimes we offer to help people one time. What stops us from helping more than one person, more than once? Why not reach many people, many times, by using your time, talent and treasures? Don't have the attitude that because you have helped someone once, you say, "Now, you are on your own."

Harriet Tubman led 300 former slaves to freedom and she never lost one. "Her train never derailed nor did she lose one passenger."

Go back and help someone learn how to fly again; to realize they have the eagle spirit in them. They have gotten down and discouraged, they have lost their way, they have given up. They are not aware that they were designed "to fly not to fall, to climb not to crawl, to soar and not to sink." In *How To Fly Like An Eagle With Wings Like A Wimp!* I emphasize what it is going to take for *you* to learn how to fly again.

BONUS FROM JONAS
"The caterpillar has a lot of legs! No matter how fast it runs...It will never fly unless it is transformed into a butterfly!"

This book will help you to be transformed into the eagle that you were designed and destined to be by God. It is your time to mount up with wings like an Eagle and fly high in the sky. Fly above mediocrity; fly above "I can't;" fly above your circumstances; fly above blaming others; fly above lack of education; fly above the pigment of your skin; fly above your economic status; fly above low self-esteem; fly High Eagle! And take someone with you!

Let me share one final story with you. There was an eagle, a chicken, an owl, and a sparrow. The challenge was to see which one could fly the highest.

The chicken took off, and he flew just a little bit higher than the ground and said, "I'm a chicken. I'm not supposed to be up here flying." So the chicken came down. Next the owl took off and said, "Who, me? I'm not supposed to be up here." So the owl came down.

Finally, the eagle and the sparrow took off. The eagle went soaring higher and higher as only an eagle can, and this eagle just kept on going, gliding high above the horizon. Then, all of a sudden the sparrow shot up above the eagle, and the eagle was amazed.

The eagle said to the sparrow, "In all my life, I have never seen a bird that is able to fly higher than I can. How did you do it?" And the sparrow said to the eagle, "It was easy, you see, the whole time I was on your back."

So the moral of that story is:

How To Fly Like an Eagle With Wings Like a Wimp!

The eagle gave the sparrow a ride on its back. The eagle helped the sparrow, just as you can help someone else soar to their greatest heights. As each of you fly to new levels of life especially after having read this book, I challenge you as eagles to fly high, and to take somebody with you.

I like what former president, Theodore Roosevelt once said: "I choose not to be a common man. It's my right to be uncommon if I can. I seek opportunity not security. I do not wish to be a kept citizen; humbled and dulled by having the state look after me. I want to take the calculated risk to dream, and to build. To fail and to succeed. I refuse to live from hand to mouth. I prefer the challenges of life to guaranteed existence; the thrill of fulfillment to the state calm of utopia. I will never cower before any master, nor bend to any friend. It is my heritage to stand erect, proud and unafraid; to think and act for myself, and face the world boldly and say, "This I have done."

I like what former Prime Minister Winston Churchill once said, "Never give up. Never, never give up." Give someone else a ride on your back. Lift someone up.

BONUS FROM JONAS
"If it's going to be, it's up to me. If you are going to get through, it's up to you!"

Let's say it again with even *greater* conviction. "If it's going to be, it's up to me.

If you are going to get through, it's up to you."

BONUS FROM JONAS
"Never give up! Never give in! And Never give out! Because it is always too early to quit. Because a quitter never wins and a winner never quits."

I like what Amelia Earhart, the great woman aviator, said: "Some of us have runways already built for us. If you have one. Take Off. But if you do not have one, then understand: It is *your* responsibility to grab a shovel, and to build one for yourself. And for all those who will follow you!"
In my book, *How To Fly Like An Eagle With Wings Like A Wimp!,* I, Jonas Gadson, known as "Mr. Enthusiastic!", have given to you the tools, proven techniques that will help you to live your dreams, goals, and aspirations through "education, inspiration, and motivation." I challenge and charge you as eagles to fly high, to have that **E**yesight, to have the proper **A**ttitude, to fly to the **Greatness** that is within you, to allow yourselves **L**aughter and joy on the journey, and to be willing to go the **E**xtra mile.

This is the Eagle call. Join me now!

"Mount up with wings like an Eagle!"

BONUS FROM JONAS
"We are on our way to the top and we cannot be stopped!"

Let us live our dreams, our goals and our aspirations. Let us meet the challenge and fly to higher heights that we never dreamed of. Will *you* take the challenge? Now is *your* time. Will you achieve more than ever before?

Fly, eagles, fly! And take someone else with you.

Always remember...

BONUS FROM JONAS
"There's no defense against Greatness!
If there is a crack then Greatness will seep through...
If there is no crack, then Greatness will break through!"

"Since Greatness Is Possible Excellence Is Not Enough!
Go For Greatness!"

Interview from Bruce Eaton's book, *Conquering Your Financial Stress*

Jonas Gadson is poised to become one of the top motivational speakers in the country. Known as "Mr. Enthusiastic" the message on his answering machine alone will pump you up. But equally inspirational as one of Jonas' speeches is his personal story: How he set his own course for learning that has taken him far beyond even his own initial expectations. Now in his early forties, Jonas went directly from high school in South Carolina to working on an assembly line in a manufacturing plant in Rochester, New York. By 1975, he had settled into a similar position with Eastman Kodak Company.

As the years rolled along, Jonas felt increasingly bogged down by the repetition of his work. "In 1980, he woke up to the fact that no matter who I worked for, I couldn't expect Corporate America to do for me the things I needed to do for myself. College isn't for everyone, but learning is. You can't control your job security. You can create skill security."

Jonas began an intensive and self-directed program on self-improvement, absorbing videos, tapes, and books on his own time and attending evening classes on a consistent basis. By 1989, he had the confidence to pursue his vision: becoming a motivational speaker. Long-involved with charity work, Jonas had helped raise over $1 million dollars for Rochester's underprivileged. But all of his speaking experience was within the church.

"I had to start over and learn how to deliver my message in a way that would permit me to speak anywhere. In front of any audience. So I began my journey."

Jonas joined the National Speakers Association and Toast-masters International. Winning contests and becoming an Area Governor in the organization. Seeking out the best speakers in the business for advice, he spoke at every opportunity. And with experience came recognition. The requests for his presentations began to grow, from inner-city churches to elite private schools and corporate boardrooms.

Jonas now makes over 100 speeches a year around the country. His signature speech is "How to Fly Like An Eagle With Wings Like A Wimp!" He now has his own weekly radio show, "Partners for Purposeful Living." In the works: a video, a book, and expanding his show to a daily broadcast.

"I am investing in my dreams," Jonas explains. "Money is a tool. Unfortunately, too many people love money and use people, instead of loving people and using money. I tell entrepreneurs that if they are getting into business just to make money, I will save them the trip. They won't make it. You have got to love something so much that you are willing to do it for free. And that's what will make you good enough to get paid."

All the while preparing himself for the future opportunities as a public speaker, Jonas has become a specialist in quality control at Kodak. "One day the company initiated a diversity training program. I knew that the program was perfect for me to use my skills, and that I was more than ready to make a positive difference. I said, "Let me try. People looked at me like I was crazy. They had no idea what I was working on outside the plant."

Jonas shattered the preconceived mold for a corporate trainer on his way to becoming the 1995–1996 Eastman Kodak Trainer of the Year. More than 5,000 of his fellow employees from 69 countries and from janitors to vice presidents have benefited from the knowledge and skills he developed bit by bit on his own time, turning spare hours into ability.

When Jonas puts his charge into his audiences and brings them to their feet, I guarantee you that no-one hesitates or sits on his hands while pondering Jonas' background...He is Great at what he does. And that's what really counts. And the key to his success is his vision of his classroom: all of life, 24 hours a day. And truly believing his motto:

"Since Greatness Is Possible, Being Excellent Is Not Enough!"

Mr. Gadson was interviewed by Mr. Bruce Eaton, Author of *Conquering Your Financial Stress;* 30,000 copies were published and sold in bookstores nationwide.

"If You Think It. Ink It! Write It Down and Then Get It Done!"

Notes

Resources

    1. References on the Eagle: These are the three websites where some of the information we are using in this book about the eagle were found:

- http://www.wildlifedepartment.com/fastfacts.htm. Oklahoma Department of Wildlife Conservation
- http://www.enchantedlearning.com/subjects/birds/info/eagle.shtm/
- http://jmm.aaa.net.au/articles/2982.htm. The Raptor Center. University of Minnesota, Jennifer Vieth, Assist. Curator.

    2. All scriptural references used in this book have been taken from the King James Version of the Bible. (KJV)

    3. Resources used in this book are listed below by chapter.

Jonas Gadson Autobiography
    1. Gullah Language and Culture; Coastalguide.com; News.Nationalgeographic.com, "Gullah Culture in Danger of Fading Away," by Dahleen Glanton, *Chicago Tribune,* June 8, 2001.

Chapter 1
    2. The number of people who lost their lives on the Titanic when it sank: 1,523. *Encyclopedia Titanica,* www.encyclopediatitanica.org.

    3. Twenty people who lost their lives from the February 2, 2007, tornado in Lady Lakes, Florida. Tornado in Lady Lake County, Florida. Charleston Daily Mail Newspaper. February 8, 2007. The Associated Press.

4. The comeback of the bald eagle in America. 10,000 pairs in 2007 "Bald Eagle Soars Off Endangered List" June 28, 2007. www.cbsnews.com/stories/2007/06/28/tech/main.

5. The population of America on September 16, 2010, was 310,265,599 people. US Population. US World Population Clocks. US Census Bureau. www. census.gov/main/www/popclock.html.

Chapter 3

6. Nelson Mandela. The Nelson Mandela Foundation 2010. www.nelsonmandela.org.

7. Iraq-Afghanistan War. As of September 16, 2010, 5,698 American soldiers have lost their lives in the wars in Iraq and Afghanistan.; www.icasualties.org/oef.

8. US Young People. Population. US Census 2007 American Community Survey. American Fact Finder for US Demographics.

9. Hurricane Katrina. 1800 lives lost. Surviving Katrina. Facts About Katrina. Discovery Channel. http://dsc.discovery.com/convergence/katrina/facts/facts.html.

10. United States Unemployment. Bureau of Labor Statistics (202) 691-7391. www.bls.gov. US Dept. of Labor. Unemployment Rate. Quarterly from 1948–2010. 1983. 10.4 -10.1(1st-4th Quarter) http://research.stlouisfed.ogr/fred2/data/UNRate.txt. www.bls.gov/newsrelease/empsit.nr0. htm. The August 2010 Bureau of Labor Statistics Report lists the number of Americans out of work at 14.9 million.

11. Civil Rights Act of 1964. www.America.gov. Engaging the World. March on Washington. www.pbs.org/newshour/extra/teachers.

Chapter 4

1. United States Unemployment Rates. Bureau of Labor Statistics April 2, 2010. (202) 691-7391. www.bls.gov/news.release/empsit.nr0.htm.

2. United States Housing Foreclosures. www.ResponsibleLending.org

3. Health Insurance. Census Bureau Report Sept. 10, 2009. "Income Poverty & Health Insurance Coverage in the US 2008." On March 23, 2010, President Barack Obama Signed into law the Patient Protection & Affordable Care Act. www.whitehouse.gov.

4. Number of Small Businesses. US Dept of Commerce 2007, 2008. The 2009 SBA Small Business Economy Report. www.sba.gov/advocacy. Non-employer firms are entities with business receipts of at least $1,000 but without paid employees. (Census Bureau Definition).

5. Literacy. National Institute for Literacy. www.nifl.gov. NALS Survey 2003 and Census Bureau Report 2007.

6. Poverty. United States Census Bureau Report Sept. 10, 2009. "Income, Poverty and Health Insurance Coverage in the US 2008" Report; National Center for Children in Poverty; 2007 Report and World Health Organization.

7. World Hunger. World Health Organization www.who.int. and Bread for the World. www.bread.org.

8. United States Obesity. Journal of the American Medical Association. Jan. 23, 2010.

9. Teen-Aged Pregnancy. Centers for Disease Control 2009. National Institutes of Health 2009. Health and Human Service Administration Office of Population Affairs Clearing-House (204) 453-2800. www.hhs.gov/opa.

10. Self-Esteem. National Association of Self-Esteem. www.self-esteem-nase.org/research.

11. Drug Abuse. Drug Abuse Statistics. Center for Disease Control. 2007 National Survey on Drug Use and Health. Office of Applied Sciences.

12. Suicide in the United States. National Institute of Mental Health. Suicide in the US. 2009 Fact Sheet.

13. High School Drop Out Rate. Institute for Education Sciences. US Dept of Ed. Sept. 2009 Northeastern University. Boston, MA. www.clms.neu.edu

14. Teen Violence. Illinois Council Against Handgun Violence – (312) 341-0939. www. ichv.org.

15. Cancer in United States. American Cancer Society Inc. Cancer Facts & Figures 2008, US News & World Report May 27, 2009; National Cancer Institute SEER Reports 2010 www.seer.cancer.gov

16. Prison population. US Bureau of Justice Statistics 2009; US Bureau of Justice Statistics. CNN article. Crime Watch. March 2, 2009. www.infoplease.com, Justice Policy Institute 2002.

17. Sept. 11, 2001 Tragedy. www.CNN.com/specials/2001/trade.center/victims/www.CNN.com/2010/US/0911/September.aa.anniversary/index.html.

18. Iraqi & Afghanistan wars. www.icasualties.org/oef.

19. American Tragedy at Fort Hood, Texas. www.CNN.com/2009/crime/11/06/texas.forthoodshootings.

20. Earthquake in Haiti. Death toll. Associated Press. Thursday Feb. 11, 2010. www.ap.org

Chapter 5

12. The Anatomy of an Illness as Perceived by the Patient. Reflections on Healing by Dr. Norman Cousins.

Chapter 6

13. Obama's Acceptance Speech, "This Is Your Victory." Tuesday, November 4, 2008. www.CNN.com.

14. US Population on September 16, 2010, was 310,265,599 people. US Population. US World Population Clocks. US Census Bureau. www. census.gov/main/www/ popclock.html.

About the Author

Jonas Gadson, DTM, known as "Mr. Enthusiastic!" is a Nationally-Known Motivational Speaker, Certified Trainer, Consultant, Radio Personality, Author, and Ordained Minister. He is President and CEO of Jonas Gadson Unlimited. A Corporate Training Company specializing in "Speaking, Training and Developing Greatness!" He is committed to helping people develop their personal and professional Greatness!

His motto is: "Since Greatness Is Possible Excellence Is Not Enough! Go For Greatness!" He trained 8,000 employees from 69 countries at Eastman Kodak Company. He delivered his signature speech entitled, "How To Fly Like An Eagle With Wings Like A Wimp!" to 500 people from around the world at Toastmasters International Convention in St. Louis, Missouri. He received a standing ovation and his message stayed on the organization's Best Selling list for two consecutive years! He brings over 30 years of corporate knowledge, skills, expertise and experience from Xerox Corporation and Eastman Kodak Company to the speaking and training arenas.

Mr. Gadson, a graduate of Beaufort High School, has been selected and was inducted into the Beaufort High School Alumni Hall of Fame on October 22, 2010, for distinguishing himself in profession, leadership, and service! "We are proud to claim you as a Beaufort Eagle!"

He is a graduate of Dale Carnegie Training where he was selected twice to help train other corporate professionals. He is a member of Toastmasters International (DTM), which is the highest level of achievement in this organization. Very few ever accomplish the DTM designation out of over 260,000 members worldwide.

He is an Accomplished Communicator and 1st Place Winner of many Oratorical Contests. He was Distinguished President, Distinguished Area Governor, and a Charter Member of the High Noon Toastmasters Club in Rochester, New York, that has earned Distinguished Club recognition every year since its inception. He is a mentor for the Leadership and Public Speaking Toastmasters Club in Beaufort, South Carolina.

He is an Internationally Published Author having two articles published in Sharing Ideas Magazine, the largest professional speakers' magazine in the world: "How to Be Brilliant in the Basics" and "Dare to Dream and Then Do It!" He was also featured in the book, Conquering Your Financial Stress by Bruce Eaton. Thirty thousand copies were published nationwide.

Mr. Gadson has been interviewed on radio programs across the country. He was interviewed twice on Financially Speaking Radio, WBNW 1120 AM, hosted by Mrs. Paige Stover-Hague, reaching an audience of 600,000 affluent listeners throughout Southeastern Massachusetts and Cape Cod. He hosted three of his own radio programs, one of which was entitled 'Partners for Purposeful Living.' He has spoken to millions of people across the country and around the world on radio and over the internet.

Mr. Gadson has a Corporate background and has spoken for numerous Fortune 500 Companies and Corporations; Eastman Kodak Company, Adelphi Automotive, Strong Memorial Hospital, Rochester Business Men, Avon, Rochester Women's Network, South Carolina Eligibility Workers Association, Orangeburg Department of Mental Health, for the National Society of Black Engineers Conference – Charlotte, NC, the Jesuit Boys School – Rochester, New York, the C-STEP and STEP Programs at Syracuse University – Syracuse, New York, the Gear Up Program – Milwaukee, Wisconsin, Beaufort Youth Conference, Technical College of the LowCountry – African American Boys & Men Mentoring Program, Battle Creek High School and additional schools and colleges all across the country, non-profit organizations, and churches.

He is a member of the Hilton Head/Bluffton Chamber of Commerce where he was featured in 'Members Making News,' Chamber Business Monthly – June 2009. He is also a member of the Beaufort Regional Chamber of Commerce in Beaufort, South Carolina and TNT Professional Networking in Rochester, New York.

He is a former member of the National Speakers Association, the Black Business Association of Rochester, and FraserNet.

He is a graduate of the Excellence In Speaking Institute with Ty Boyd, Charlotte, North Carolina.

He is a graduate of the International Leadership Institute, Nassau, Bahamas.

He is a graduate of 'Live Your Speaking Dreams'; a speaker's and author's boot camp in Tampa, Florida.

Mr. Gadson is the Minister of the Beaufort Church of Christ in Beaufort, South Carolina.

His Motto Is:

**"Since Greatness Is Possible Excellence Is Not Enough!
Go For Greatness!"**

Products and Services

Jonas Gadson delivers Dynamic Motivational Speeches, Keynotes, Seminars and Workshops on the following Topics: Motivation, Self-Esteem, Leadership, Communication, Team-Building, Sales, and Diversity.

Products are available for purchase that will help you continue to develop your personal and professional Greatness! A MUST have for your personal and professional development library.

Book: "How To Fly Like An Eagle With Wings Like A Wimp!" $19.95 + $5.95 shipping/handling

Signature Speech: "How To Fly Like An Eagle with Wings Like A Wimp!" Delivered by the author to 500 people from around the world at Toastmasters International Convention at the Adams Mark Hotel in St. Louis, Missouri, where he earned a standing ovation. (1 hour 4 min. long)

- How To Fly Like An Eagle with Wings Like A Wimp! CD
- How To Fly Like An Eagle With Wings Like A Wimp! DVD
- How To Fly Like An Eagle With Wings Like A Wimp! Video Classic
- How To Fly Like An Eagle With Wings Like A Wimp! Cassette

If you are looking for an "educational, inspirational and motivational speaker" for your next event – Look No Further! Call "Jonas with the Bonus!" NOW!

(843) 838-3853 * jg@jonasbonus.com

Motivational Speaker
Keynote Speaker
Workshop Presenter
Seminar Presenter
Master of Ceremonies

To contact him by mail, write:

Partners for Purposeful Living
P.O. Box 629 Beaufort, SC 29906
(843) 838-3853
jg@jonasbonus.com
www.jonasbonus.com

His motto is:

**"Since Greatness Is Possible Excellence Is Not Enough!
Go For Greatness!"**

LaVergne, TN USA
09 December 2010
208086LV00006B/3/P